INCLUSIVITY AND INSTITUTIONAL CHANGE
IN EDUCATION

THEOLOGICAL EDUCATION BETWEEN THE TIMES

Ted A. Smith, series editor

Theological Education between the Times gathers diverse groups of people for critical, theological conversations about the meanings and purposes of theological education in a time of deep change. The project is funded by the Lilly Endowment Inc.

Daniel O. Aleshire
Beyond Profession: The Next Future of Theological Education

Elizabeth Conde-Frazier
Atando Cabos: Latinx Contributions to Theological Education

Keri Day
Notes of a Native Daughter: Testifying in Theological Education

Willie James Jennings
After Whiteness: An Education in Belonging

Mark D. Jordan
Transforming Fire: Imagining Christian Teaching

Maria Liu Wong
On Becoming Wise Together: Learning and Leading in the City

Colleen Mary Mallon, OP
Inclusivity and Institutional Change in Education: A Theologian's Journey

Ted A. Smith
The End of Theological Education

Chloe T. Sun
Attempt Great Things for God: Theological Education in Diaspora

Amos Yong
Renewing the Church by the Spirit: Theological Education after Pentecost

Mark S. Young
The Hope of the Gospel: Theological Education and the Next Evangelicalism

INCLUSIVITY AND INSTITUTIONAL CHANGE IN EDUCATION

A Theologian's Journey

Colleen Mary Mallon, OP

WILLIAM B. EERDMANS PUBLISHING COMPANY

GRAND RAPIDS, MICHIGAN

2024-05

Wm. B. Eerdmans Publishing Co.
4035 Park East Court SE, Grand Rapids, Michigan 49546
www.eerdmans.com

Published 2024
Printed in the United States of America

30 29 28 27 26 25 24   1 2 3 4 5 6 7

ISBN 978-0-8028-7896-0

Library of Congress Cataloging-in-Publication Data

A catalog record for this book is available from the Library
of Congress.

To my beloved sister,
Mary Mallon-Behrens,
whose life illumines and inspires mine
and whose truth always calls me to more

Contents

Acknowledgments

I am deeply grateful for the gift of belonging to an amazing group of theological colleagues, called together by Ted Smith, to contribute to phase two of Theological Education between the Times (TEBT): Amos Yong, Chloe Sun, Daniel Aleshire, Elizabeth Conde-Frazier, Hoffsman Ospino, Keri Day, Lucila Crena, Maria Liu Wong, Mark Jordan, Mark Young, Rachelle Green, Willie J. Jennings, and Ted Smith along with our editor, Ulrike (Uli) Guthrie. I can still feel the effervescent joy bubbling inside me after our first gathering at Emory University. Our prayer, risk taking, and engagement with each other coming from such different theological commitments; our conversations over meals; and our mutual yes to become a writing community thrilled me beyond any postdoctoral scholarly gathering I had known. Colleague-friends, I learn so much from you, and I continue to reflect with gratitude on our treasured times at Emory, Esperanza College, City Seminary of New York, and Serra Retreat, Malibu. Thank you for your amazing contributions to this series. I am humbled to be in your wise and joyful company.

As you will learn, dear reader, the invitation to join TEBT came at a pivotal moment in my journey as a theological educator. The original request, which was to write about doing formative theology with Catholic health-care executives leading a ministry of the church, shifted dramatically for me on the heels of an unanticipated job change. The book you are holding came to be because of the consummate, compassionate listening of our amazing editor, Ulrike Guthrie, who literally "heard me" into a new moment. Uli, you helped me to have the courage to let go of what was so as to embrace the opportunity of writing, in real time, my own "in-between" story of doing theology. Benefiting from Ted Smith's generous scholarly-pastoral hospitality (yes, all that, Ted!), I was able to embrace a new invitation and bring this book forth. Uli and Ted, I am profoundly indebted to both of you. Thank you from my heart.

Many other people have also supported me on this journey. Profound gratitude goes to Christina Hale-Elliott, who offered her passionate leadership in equity education to our community and who graced me as a compassionate, truth-speaking mentor. Special thanks to the sisters of my local community and my colleagues in ministry, who have honored and provided space to do this writing. I will hold my writing weeks at Villa Maria del Mar in Santa Cruz, California, in special memory always. Thank you to the sisters and lay colleagues at the Villa who made those days so productive and joyous. Living the deeper lessons of right relationship has happened for me in the company of friends who continuously offer me grace in struggles and sanctuary in suffering: Carolyn McCormack, OP; Janice Therese Wellington, OP; Joye Gros, OP; Kathleen McManus, OP; Maribeth Howell, OP; Michelle Besmer, Paula Kaintz, Reina Perea, OP, sisters of my heart all. Thank you for your love. And I give thanks for my family, particularly my mother, Rita Mallon, who never stops praying for me and my ministry. And for my dear sister, Mary Mallon-Behrens, to whom I dedicate this book about embodying truth.

This book recounts the ongoing journey of a Roman Catholic sister theologian caught in multiple, overlapping episodes of being "in between," all very much still in process. I offer these moments to you, dear reader, well aware of their "yet to be" dimensions, especially from within the ministries I currently serve. And while most of the names of the folks working these ministries, my colleagues, remain unshared for reasons of privacy, I want my sisters and my ministry partners to know of my deep gratitude for their patience with my learning curves; for their engagement with our commitment to live *veritas*, the gospel of Jesus, from the historical "in betweens" that are uniquely ours; and for their own amazing contributions to the transformation of our community. Thank you for humbly and reverently embracing the task of embodying *veritas* each day.

Episode 1

Beginning

... to make an end is to make a beginning.

—T. S. Eliot[1]

Embodying veritas—the matter of how to live out or embody truth—and writing a book on this subject became my particular focus in late 2020 when a pink slip suddenly terminated my career as a theological educator . . . or so it seemed at the time. Given the ongoing, precarious financial circumstances of stand-alone theological schools, the surprise of my termination was less about "the why" and more about "the how." This was my how:

> *Dear Colleen,*
> *I am sending you this email . . .*
> *made the decision to terminate . . .*
> *your*
> *Associate Professor position . . .*
> *due to the current financial conditions . . .*
> *plan accordingly to seek other employment . . .*

Receiving this email message was a jolting experience. I had worked happily, even passionately, for this institution for over ten years and had contributed significantly to its sustainable future.

1

Though my school administration's transgression of its own written policy regarding termination of faculty contracts clearly disturbed me, once I caught my breath from the most immediate shock, this push into the "in between" was not entirely unwelcome. I am a theologian and a woman religious, a member of the Order of Preachers (Dominicans), who also sponsor that school of theology. The institution's evolving journey during my tenure had seen four presidents in just over ten years. Caught by an institutional "in between," the school's latest administration appeared to be stepping back from what had been, in the school's prime, its notable reputation as a place of dialogue, inclusion, and community.

Electronic pink slips are a clear indicator of this change. It was very strange and awkward to explain to my sisters, particularly to the women who lead my religious community, how I lost my job. As is true of our lay counterparts, our incomes support our "family" of sisters and our other ministries. We count on working well into our so-called retirement years. This pink slip effectively ended that part of my career.

While I knew that I could serve effectively in a different educational or pastoral setting, that pink slip also put me face-to-face with the end of a time that had been both precious and productive for me as a theologian and a formator. I received a great deal from those years, including, for a time, the friendship of some wonderful colleagues. The experiences of those years have helped me to navigate this new moment and to have and share with you my own theological education in the new in-between spaces.

Many threshold crossings into liminal, in-between spaces come to us as such uninvited or pink-slip invitations. Perhaps my experience brings to mind some of your own pink-slip moments, whether professional, romantic, or health- or business-related. If so, then you know this feeling of: Well, here we are, caught in the unexpected, facing new circumstances and unanticipated horizons. To get to the stage of acceptance of our new reality is a big journey, as you know. No wonder that "taking a long, loving look at what is real" is a spiritual practice that requires significant cultivation! Can we accept what is, make the shift, and move on? And going deeper: Does curiosity or resentment fuel our acceptance? Or perhaps a little of each?

On my own journey from being pink-slipped to finding acceptance and a new calling, I've found that it really does matter which of these two energies—curiosity or resentment— accompanies our response to being pushed into unexpected between spaces. If we can manage to center ourselves into an attentive curiosity and carefully surrender our resentment, we might find our "in between" to be a sacred space where we are "undergoing God" (to borrow the words of theologian James Alison).[2] Alison chooses the verb "undergo" because while there is a passivity to it (we are literally being acted upon by God), there is also an element of us willingly *allowing* God to act on us. We could after all choose otherwise. We could resist.

It is a discernment, isn't it—this figuring out whether what we are undergoing is "of God" or not? We might ask: Where has God been in those moments, particularly moments in the theological academy, when misunderstanding, mean-spiritedness, jealousy, and envy have interrupted the good that could have been in a situation, a decision, a program? Are we undergoing God or undergoing human sinfulness, our own and others?

Pondering that question, I realize that I can distinguish but not separate the two. By God's own design, this sojourn is an incarnational journey in which the promise given in Christ Jesus is one of divine accompaniment and friendship in the best of times and the worst of times.

So, for me, getting and dealing with my pink slip was an "undergoing God" moment.

I sat in the convent chapel as I reread the email. And while the bizarreness of receiving a so-called pink slip via email was not lost on me, a moment of prayer descended, and in my mind's eye I saw myself as a small child, standing in front of a massive, worn wooden door with a large knocker. The child me was trying to reach up, to knock on the door and be allowed in. . . . I could not reach it. And then, an intuition simply invited me to turn away from the door, to turn around. To my amazement and delight, there was a vast, verdant, sun-kissed valley before me. It was beautiful, lush, green, light-filled, and drenched with freshness. The call came clearly: "Allow the door to close. It is time to turn. I am doing something new. Meet me there."

Meeting God at that threshold moment and crossing over into a new space for doing theology continues to be personally transformative, as you'll soon see.

I am a leader, and in my past institutions I have led several important initiatives with creativity, passion, intelligence, and tenacious hard work. I know how to operate on a shoestring budget. I enjoy the shared energy of good teamwork. And I have high expectations of those who partner with me on a project. I recognize that some of the lessons that have come to me are ones that I have invited by my conscious and unconscious behaviors. And my experience has been that God meets me there, in the struggle, in the learning, in the leaning in, and also in the suffering of betrayal, in the disaster of self-doubt, in the disappointment of discovering that people are not always able to be who they represent themselves to be.

I am not really good with people and situations that are fraught with drama. Maybe it was my upbringing, my straight-arrow dad who lost work because he could not pretend not to see the wrong that was happening on the job. Sometimes I hear myself and realize that I am channeling "Dad energy" again: authoritative, directive, and fiery. That is not always helpful. Those who know and love me recognize that I hold two strong, seemingly opposite dynamisms in my spirit: I am both deeply kind and thoroughly choleric. Like most of us, I have been profoundly shaped by my family of origin. My inner dynamics, holding both the kindness and the anger, has offered me lots of practice when it comes to the mystery of human relationships. I can jump to trust too quickly, with the result of being painfully disappointed. And I know I can drive people crazy, either by being viewed as naively optimistic or conversely by being absolutely "dogged" in my pursuit of something of which I refuse to let go.

For me, undergoing God in this midlife moment has been an experience of entering into the mystery of my own unfolding self-discovery, the places where I am strong and the places where I am wounded, self-inflicted or otherwise. On this journey, I am learning how to acknowledge the hurt and the harm and seek healing. The child in me is getting much better at accepting people as they are. It took me a long time to realize that some of the unconscious expectations that I believed and held only added to my suffering. Maybe you have learned this, too, on your journeys. In a book, one of my favorite spiritual writers and practitioners, David Richo, lists five things that we cannot change in life.[3] Revisiting this list after being let go from my teaching position has helped me to accept the way things are and to move forward.

> Everything changes and ends.
> Things do not always go according to plan.
> Life is not fair.
> Pain is part of life.
> People are not loving and loyal all the time.

I think the last statement about people not being loyal and loving all the time has been the hardest one for me to integrate. And at the same time, it has been important for me to own that for other people, *I have not been loving and loyal all the time*, either. The prolonged act of undergoing the graces of allowing, accepting, and remaining curious about "Why? and "What next?" is etching on my person important virtues in which I still need much practice: owning my impact, not just my intention; embracing a new depth of humility and recognizing its repeated absence; making space for discomfort and lack of closure; and unlearning control to welcome a discerning heart.

Each of these virtues is a bodily practice of presence. Together they are ways in which I am learning how to show up in the world in a new way . . . all because of a closed door, a pink slip, and the necessity of having to pivot—to what I did not yet know.

5

How about you? What have been the significant closed doors, pink-slip moments, and pivots you've had to make in your theological journey/ career? (Feel free to jot down some responses.)

How are you "undergoing God" right now? In the process, what virtues is divine Love etching on your person?

Particularly if you are currently at some kind of a transitional moment of your life, what hopes do you have for your personal transformation, future growth, and practice?

* * *

Fast-forward a couple of years after that pink slip: How am I "undergoing God" right now?

Well, I continue to walk through a significant transition time or threshold crossing, and this book is the story—my story—of stepping into the invitation to be "in between the times." In terms of undergoing God, the book is a chronicle of what I have learned and what I am continuing to learn about doing theology in the in-between spaces. It is about learning to see a still-wider institutional context in which theological education happens now. It is about spaces like a Catholic high school, caught and called out in the between of a "tipping point" moment (defined by a global pandemic, the murder of George Floyd, the rise of Black Lives Matter, the call for full LGBTQ+ rights), and now repenting for its complicity in racial inequity and other forms of systemic aggression and bias. It is about spaces like an entire system of Catholic schools now wanting to create real cultural change to instantiate the gospel of Jesus. And it is about spaces like a community of Catholic women religious navigating new understandings of right relationship among themselves, with their lay partners and their various ministries.

These highly particular in-between spaces correspond to the large-scale reckoning we are all in the midst of right now as a nation. When social upheaval reaches a tipping point, we should expect nothing less. The murder of George Floyd was a tipping point that exposed the scourge of our country's unhealed racial wounds. In those nine minutes, white Americans saw clearly what we have rendered invisible and what persons of color deal with every single day: white privilege and white supremacy. That murder, that tipping point, forced us as a nation to pull back the blinds on how whiteness fuels and perpetuates anti-Black violence. And if we choose to stay with what we can no longer deny, then we might rightly ask:

On what social guarantees was Derek Chauvin counting as he knelt on the carotid artery of George Floyd for over nine minutes?

From what ingrained bias was Amy Cooper acting when she made a false police complaint against Christian Cooper, a Black man and birdwatcher who asked her to leash her dog in Central Park as required by law?

What were the conditions that made the racially motivated murder of Ahmaud Arbery by three white men conceivable and possible?

The breadth and the depth of the injustices that white privilege/ supremacy has masked, silenced, pushed down, and repeatedly denied erupted in May 2020, and the aftershocks continue to be felt. George Floyd's death, among others, exposed white supremacy in all its lethal reality.[4]

For me and for many of my Dominican sisters, the murder of George Floyd stands alone as a turning point. In that moment, we experienced the incontrovertible evidence of the structural racism that protects white privilege *and* promotes anti-Black violence. Years ago, Jamie Phelps, one of my Dominican sisters from

Adrian, Michigan, gently admonished me never to forget that the flip side of racism is white privilege. Twenty years later, I am still learning Jamie's prescient words. I believe beyond a shadow of a doubt that Derek Chauvin would never have knelt on the neck of a white man for one minute, let alone nine minutes. And that is what makes being Black and brown in America so traumatic and terrifying.

My personal work of becoming an antiracist daily challenges my false consciousness and my complicity. I am learning to accept with a new humility my regular self-encounters with false consciousness and failures to be a true ally—all the opportunities I missed to resist the structures of my unmerited privilege. Yes, I am still that person who struggles to know what to say when a "good" white person commits microaggressions. I fail to act because it doesn't serve to embarrass an otherwise good person impolitely: "She didn't really mean it that way." I will spend the rest of my life unlearning my privilege and resisting with accountable compassion the bias that racism imposes on perceptions. After all, I do not see, feel, or experience what people of color see, feel, and experience on a daily basis.

Two recent experiences suggest how much I have yet to learn. The first was a faculty and staff in-service session devoted to understanding and responding to microaggressions in the classroom. Several of the examples that were shared triggered one of the white faculty members. The white instructor became quite emotional, expressing both frustration and anxiety about the material. *Isn't this all a bit overmuch? Isn't this what happens to all adolescents? Nobody gets through high school unscathed. Why are we making a big deal about what is just kids being kids and learning how to grow up?* The sharing escalated emotionally, even as the in-service facilitator attempted to respond. A second faculty member, a person of color, challenged with authority and clarity the assertions that the first (white) person had outlined: *There is no such thing as color blindness. A person of color is constantly evaluating their environment for indicators of acceptance, the ability to be fully themselves or the lack thereof. Failing to understand this and to address this harm has serious learning outcomes for our students.*

The white teacher left the Zoom meeting clearly distressed.

My own lesson came when I debriefed with our presenter. I shared that we were reaching out to the distressed educator, recognizing that something else might have triggered such strong negative reactions to the training. Our presenter asked me if we had also reached out to check on the well-being of the teacher of color. No, we had not thought of that.

There it was.
My assumption that we had to lean into the pain
of a distressed white teacher
and could be assured that our hearty, seasoned
teacher of color was just fine.

It simply did not dawn on me that I should attend to the person who appeared to me to be so confident, clear, and self-assured. I learned that day that every intervention a person of color makes in defense of justice comes at a personal cost of energy, self-care, and public perception.

My second learning experience came while reading an article in the *National Catholic Reporter.* Bryan Massingale, an African American priest and moral theologian, offered a powerful analysis of what was really at play in the incident that occurred between Amy Cooper and Christian Cooper in Central Park. You will recall that Amy Cooper, a white woman, falsely reported that she was being threatened with harm by Christian Cooper, a Black birdwatcher who simply asked her to leash her dog, as required in the park. Midway through Bryan's article, I closed my eyes and shook my head. While I am so grateful that Bryan wrote this article, I recognized that I should have written that article. I and a whole host of white theologians who have been in conversations about race, theology, and social life for years were the ones who could have, and no doubt should have, written that article. I wonder what it would have meant to Bryan if we had. Might he breathe more peacefully among us, his colleagues, knowing that we really do "get it"? There it was again—my failure to see what I was theologically equipped to do and yet failed to do.

After the pink slip, this is my new in-between context: the context of these questions of racism and bias, my own and those that people bring to me, all of us caught in our own awakening to the violence of systemic injustice. People looking to me for the wisdom of theology to ground their new real-life initiatives in liberation and justice. They are asking me: *What does right relationship look like personally and institutionally, particularly in our ministries?* They recognize that these initiatives will trigger reactions from COVID-weary folks at both ends of the political and social spectrum. They ask: *How do we bravely preach and embody the Truth in Love while building bridges between ourselves and those whom we serve?* They know and believe that any real, transformative change must be rooted in the fertile depths of our Catholic tradition. *What gospel resources will best ground and sustain our new commitments toward becoming antiracist?*

The more I approach and engage this work, the more I recognize how crucial it is for me to be in this new location, this in-between space. Indeed, I could not be doing this important work *and* remain in a traditional theological classroom like my previous workspace. Proximity to the questions arising from the ground of experience, from the relationships, the struggles, the setbacks, and the moments of integration, make my physical presence a necessary and even central component of this work, even in the midst of a pandemic. Reflecting on my past experiences as a graduate theology professor, I note that the very thing for which I was preparing my master's students, namely, to be "frontline interpreters of the gospel" within a ministry, is now my new role, too. No longer hypothetical, no longer detached from the push and pull of living contexts, I am now the one to whom myriad folks are turning with their questions and their desires to live an authentic Christian mission in a fractured time.

This book is my story of reflecting on the call (or was it a shove? still to be determined!) to move out of traditional academic settings into an in-between space of theological education. I hope that my story speaks to your own experiences of unanticipated moments of consequence and of the grace that meets us there, for we don't have to leave a job situation as I did to be confronted by events that rearrange the furniture of our lives.

* * *

I remember the first time I saw these words and chuckled.

Change Is Good.
You Go First.

One of my MA students was giving a leadership presentation on how to guide a ministry (that is also a business) through the ups and downs of ever-evolving fiscal challenges. At the time, I was the director of the MA program in Health Care Mission, which itself had represented a career pivot of sorts, even as I remained engaged in academic theology. For I am an ecclesiologist, and I had become interested in an area of ecclesial ministry—specifically the healing ministry of Jesus—that is jam-packed with lay leaders. In Catholic health care I encountered a face of the Roman Catholic Church that I, and other theologians of the church, was somehow not considering. A colleague who had spearheaded the MA in Health Care Mission and had grown the program into a recognized "gold star" experience for lay leaders in Catholic health care had lured me into this work. Shifting into this degree program had not been hard for me because I quickly recognized how its multilevel approach provided students—mostly senior leaders in Catholic health care—with both good theology and excellent formation in the context of their sixty- to eighty-hour workweeks. Sad to say, this program no longer exists, a casualty of the market forces that have wreaked harm on so many theological programs. However, the wholeness and satisfaction of engaging students already in ministry and hungry to have their passion for meaningful work fed at a more fundamental spiritual level were life-changing for me. Integrating theology with spirituality and leadership skills for ministry taught me the truth of the maxim that "transformed people transform institutions."

When Ted Smith first asked me to contribute to this series of books on doing theological education between the times, the story I wanted to tell was the health-care mission story briefly described above. I wanted to tell that story as an ecclesiologist and as a theologian-formator. Particularly over the long haul, I had experienced the transformative power of theological reflection as the students interrogated past paradigms and claimed, and then reclaimed, metaphors that *offered them more than meaning* in an ever-challenging business context. What do I *mean* by that? I cannot think of a single participant in this MA program who did not experience at one point or another a true encounter, a meeting, with the Spirit.

Over and over we received feedback: "Sister, this class is changing me." "Sister, I am finding my home again in our church." And my favorite one: "Sister, I think that you have been plotting to make us fall in love with theology." In fact, I wanted them to do more than "fall for theology": I wanted them to fall for Jesus. I knew that, in the words of José Pagola, the Spanish priest-theologian,

> A Church formed by Christians that relate to a Jesus they do not know well—confessed once in a while in an abstract and doctrinal way, a mute Jesus that . . . does not seduce or make you fall in love, that does not touch our hearts—is a Church without a future.[5]

I continue to believe in the transformational power of such an integral education, one that fosters the formation of servant leaders who are tireless in their desire to become savvy and wise stewards of the ministry entrusted to them—so much so that I continued to work on telling that story even after the pink slip changed my location. However, after a year in a new ministry space, I realized that, though I was well into the first manuscript draft, my location had changed, and so had I. Even as my proximity to Catholic health-care spaces receded, a critical and demanding ministry context beckoned my attention and now stretches me in ways I had never anticipated.

I see the hands of the Potter and the wheel is swirling. I am wet mud being held, shaped, then reshaped, now pulled, now pushed. The Potter turns the wheel and as the hollowing happens, the hands never stop the process of massaging, shaping, forming. And again, there are days when the experience is more like what Bakerwoman God does as she kneads and punches and rolls flat the dough of me. This new way of doing theology is a visceral experience, it lives in my flesh; this divine undergoing longs for me to breathe deeply the freedom that can liberate those spaces that are too tight and verging on becoming brittle. Never before have I experienced so profoundly the alignment between what I teach and who I am. For better, for worse, the medium is the message. And the medium is my life, my flesh.

That pink slip email interrupted my first attempt at sharing my experiences of doing theology "in between the times." Yes, I tried to step back into that space to retrieve lessons and insights of those days, to continue telling that story, to finish writing that manuscript into which I had already poured so much time and heart. Perhaps you know that feeling too, whether trying to retrieve a relationship, a direction, or a passion. So perhaps you will understand that the more I tried, the more the horizon of those experiences slipped away. I had loved that time in my life. I had loved my students and my school. I had treasured my colleagues and mentors who had challenged and supported my engagement with doing theology from the ground up. Now, from a space of peace and gratitude, I (and perhaps you in your own situation) can say: "That was then, and this is now."

And what a compelling "now" it is! This new journey has me deep in a new moment, a personal "Kairos." I feel catapulted from the middle of the country (Missouri) back to the West Coast (Los Angeles), where new questions and cultural circumstances now mediate those powerful, creative fingers of the Divine acting on me. I think that is why James Alison's assertion that, unconscious or not, we are all "undergoing God" is so significant for me in this present moment.

Doing theology on the "frontlines" of a ministry has a way of inscribing the lessons of the gospel more deeply and, one hopes, indelibly, on a person if we choose to stay close to such graciousness. Honestly, it is carving out in me new spaces of both vulnerability and intimacy with my God. I am undergoing the lessons that I taught with such certainty from behind my classroom desk.

Far from being distant or removed from us in
some unreachable heaven,
God's Spirit encounters us constantly in the daily moments
of our lives.

Our faith tells us that however different the Creator is from
the creature,
that difference is not about distance.
We are in the throes of grace
that simultaneously respects our integral being with its unique
autonomy
and subtly, actively penetrates our being, inviting and animating
every potential for new life.

I am with you.

Long before I started my doctoral program, I embarked on a summer master of arts in theology (MAT) degree. As a chemistry teacher who could only afford the time to complete an MA in a summer theology program, I looked forward to those classes. I had fallen in love with studying theology. The readings, the time to reflect and to write all seemed to allow a part of my heart to sing, to "come alive" in the way that Howard Thurman articulates. One of my most precious memories is of sitting in the library at the University of San Francisco and delighting in the luscious freedom to read Yves Congar for hours. Bliss!

Well into that program, I had an oral exam with the professor. His comment left me with the impression that his observation was not necessarily a compliment. "You do your theology from your prayer, don't you?" Yes, I guess I do. As a Dominican sister, I really could not do it otherwise. How is it possible to separate out that which is most essential to your self-understanding from a deeply felt vocation to live for the truth, to live from *veritas*?

I came to my theological vocation already deeply formed and shaped by my vocation as a vowed Dominican sister. I am a "midlife" theologian, having taught high school science for fifteen years, mostly among underserved populations. My Dominican vocation is the most defining identity of my life. Even as a teen I needed to know, "Where can I find the truth?" My newly "born again" Protestant classmates in my public school seemed to have something real that my heart also wanted. My Mormon friends were also remarkable young people, so genuinely good and happy, and so true to their values. All of that attracted me and pushed me to wonder: Where might I find that as a Catholic? Youth group and special retreats, parish choir, teaching CCD (Confraternity of Christian Doctrine)— all these experiences fed a deep hunger in my young person. When I met the Dominican Sisters of Mission San Jose, I discovered to my surprise that I felt "at home."

One of the first confirmations of this for me was stepping into a convent chapel and encountering a mosaic with the word *veritas* inscribed on the wall. There it was: truth. And here I am . . . in a place with like-minded seekers who are dedicated to pursuing and living the truth, these Dominican women. I will admit that it took a while to open my heart to the idea that living celibately for the rest of my life would actually be possible. Amazingly, it has been, for the most part. Seeking truth, serving truth, and now learning how to embody truth can and does offer me a path for loving that is fulfilling and joyous, even as it challenges and humbles.

So, thank you for your curiosity and for wondering with me about what it might actually mean to embody *veritas*. In what follows, I share my journey, the ins and outs, the ups and downs of bringing theology into a new context full of significant questions about what it means to be human, about how we are called to resist evil and teach our children to do so too, and about where we have failed as an institution to be bearers of light and grace in the lives of the people we hoped to serve. It's a journey in which I ask what it means for institutions to repent of past evils, and what it means to chart a new course in the midst of controversy and deep-seated, privileged resistance. These are just a few of the questions that my story engages, and I hope that in its telling you too will find something of your challenges and concerns named and engaged.

Thank you for picking up this book and pondering its stories. They are the stories of a sister-theologian released into the between times and finding in those times renewed purpose, new vision, and an invitation to allow difficult truths to be written on her heart. Embodying *veritas*, I am learning, opens one to a new intimacy with the God revealed in the mystery of Christ himself, following his cruciform pathway into gracious union and unimagined freedom.

Episode 2

Opening

"Go to your core, Colleen, go to your core and stay strong."

With these words arising from my recent prayer, I do exactly that. I start to breathe deeply and intentionally. I exhale from my abdomen and tighten my core muscles. Placing my hand on that core contraction, I consciously reclaim my center and continue to breathe myself beyond the swirling anxiety that threatens to derail me.

Barely two years into a new ministry of shepherding diversity, equity, and inclusion initiatives at a Catholic secondary school, I find myself on edge from the personal inner work of managing all that comes with leading culture change. Ego strength is important, yes. Even more significant, however, is the willingness to recognize when personal ego pain threatens to interfere with the relational work at the heart of this Dominican mission.

"Face it, Colleen, you made a mistake; you cannot be all things to all people."
"Folks don't have to be happy with you, they have a right to their perceptions and beliefs."
"Expect conflict, it's human!"

The grace of that "Go to your core" moment stays with me now. It reminds me to pay attention to my own self-care in the face of ever-expanding ministry initiatives and the conflicts that come with trying to create a school climate that is antiracist and antibias. By reflecting on that moment again and again, I can mindfully treasure the formative character of the work I am about: how the practices I recommend to others come full circle back to me. No doubt about it: I will eventually leave this ministry a very different person than when I began.

I came to this ministry in one of our community's sponsored schools in 2020 as a part-time director of adult formation for mission—the kind of adult formation that many of you also do in a similar but slightly different fashion as seminary professors. My hope, and that of the school's leaders, was that in this role I would be able to grow and deepen our Dominican charism among the members of our school community, particularly our staff and faculty. My other part-time work was to grow our Dominican Sisters' congregational engagement with our Partners in Mission, those women and men who have become our colleagues, supporters, and friends. Our congregation intentionally construed both initiatives as "formative": growing our colleagues' and supporters' engagement with their own unique spirituality and deepening their conscious connection to our Dominican charism and mission.

The ongoing reckoning that followed the murder of George Floyd completely reframed my role as a director of adult formation for mission. Up to that moment, the significance of hiring a director of diversity, equity, and inclusion (DEI) had not dawned on the consciousness of the school's leaders or board of directors. In the light of this reality, school leaders entrusted me with the formative work of creating, directing, and sustaining mission-centered, community-wide initiatives for DEI. While a small group of faculty and staff had begun important initiatives around DEI a few years earlier, the scope of the work was now much larger and more comprehensive. Our efforts had to reach not only into but also beyond the classroom. We had to learn to become what we soon recognized we did not know how to be as a predominantly white institution (PWI). Reflecting on it now, we were not unlike those to whom Dr. Martin Luther King addressed his letter from the Birmingham jail.

I have almost reached the regrettable conclusion that the Negro's great stumbling block in the stride toward freedom is not the White Citizens Councilor or the Ku Klux Klanner but the white moderate who is more devoted to order than to justice; who prefers a negative peace which is the absence of tension to a positive peace which is the presence of justice. . . . Shallow understanding from people of good will is more frustrating than absolute misunderstanding from people of ill will. Lukewarm acceptance is much more bewildering than outright rejection.[1]

When your school motto is *Veritas*, then to deny, resist, or ignore the truth when it cries out for recognition and response is like deliberately harming your own institution. That was our experience in the aftermath of the racial reckoning of George Floyd's murder as we listened to the voices of our students and alums on "@dear Instagram" accounts. These accounts were created as what Grace Sandman calls "a different kind of love letter" to their schools from graduates and students:

Students and alumni from predominantly white prep schools created Instagram pages that offered a platform for Black, Indigenous, and people of color (BIPOC) to share and expose their experiences with racism at their institutions. Accounts of those experiences were sent . . . to the Instagram account administrators, who posted them, without using the author's [*sic*] names.[2]

Schools that seemingly touted a bias-free reputation found themselves being publicly called out by BIPOC students and alums who recounted over and over their experiences of verbal abuse, particularly the use of the N-word, as well as being dismissed and disparaged as "affirmative action decisions" because they were Black or on a sports scholarship, all of this with impunity for the aggressors, students, and adults alike. Our school's @dear Instagram account recounted similar stories of harm and hurt that had gone unacknowledged or unaddressed by us, its leaders.

Reflecting on that moment now with the benefit of hindsight, I can recall my own reaction to the @dear Instagram postings addressed to our school. Initially, I registered disbelief, anxiety, sadness, denial, and defensiveness. I thought and expressed, rather dismissively, that these posts were little more than the somewhat petty memories of disgruntled adult women who, by the way, had far too much time to spend on Instagram. I also recall a certain collective "white" damage control reaction among those of us in leadership: How can we stem the tide of this bad press and just move on?

It is more than instructive now to see how our collective disgust at the fate of George Floyd *remained completely disconnected* from our own systemic enactment of repeated biased aggressions reported by our students in the @dear Instagram posts. This was our first corporate awakening to "the smog of racism" that all of us breathe.[3] We unconsciously participate in and reinforce the very same oppressive, unchecked social structures and implicit belief systems that perpetuate death-dealing aggressions against peoples of color.

This racial reckoning at our predominantly white institution has awakened us to the intersection of our multiple privileged identities and has initiated essential conversations across our school community. Those conversations are facilitating *real, substantial, and true* transformation of our school culture. If you caught the sacramental language I just used around a Catholic understanding of Christ's presence in the Eucharist, then you will know that these DEI efforts are fundamentally grounded in our school's mission and the mission of our congregation, the Dominican Sisters of Mission San Jose, the sponsor of this educational ecclesial ministry. Our mission statement proclaims that "We, the Dominican Sisters of Mission San Jose, the Congregation of the Queen of the Holy Rosary, are called to live and proclaim Jesus Christ through evangelizing, preaching, educating, and promoting justice and peace." "Educating and promoting justice and peace" have taken on a new life in this ministry.

A MISSION WITHIN A LARGER MISSION

We the Dominican Sisters of Mission San Jose, the Congregation of the Queen of the Holy Rosary, are called to live and proclaim Jesus Christ through evangelizing, preaching, educating, and promoting justice and peace.

In the spirit of St. Dominic and of our foundress, Mother Maria Pia Backes, we witness to this call through our vowed life.

Our prayer, study, ministry and life in community empower us to participate in the mission of Jesus, especially among the young, the poor and the vulnerable.

We did not realize it then, but our school's acknowledgment of our complicity in systemic racism would have repercussions on our entire community of Dominican sisters, our congregation, in both the United States and Mexico. Though we are women vowed to live for the gospel of Jesus, we too are only beginning to recognize the engulfing smog of racism and our unquestioned presumptions of white privilege that shape our self-understandings, our relationships as sisters, and our approach to our ministries among "the young, the poor and the vulnerable." You see, while I am located in the particularity of one of our ministries, I am also supporting our sisters' efforts toward articulating a future direction for our life and ministry rooted in a renewed understanding of what it means to live in right relationship.

These two stories—the story of our school's journey toward becoming antiracist and antibias and the story of our congregation's journey into the transformative commitment to live in right relationship—are at the heart of my story as a theologian working "in the between."

In what follows, you will see how, between 2020 and 2022, these two spaces have overlapped in significant ways: both the questions raised and the impact of enacting new responses to those questions. These two stories of institutions seeking to grow in justice have supported and encouraged separate but deeply related initiatives that are seeding real change rooted in the gospel of Jesus.

The journey at school continued.

That August of 2020, as we approached a new school year, we recognized that there was no one among us equipped to teach and to guide us to see what we had not seen. There was no one among us to show us how to make amends for and to reconcile what we had unintentionally but clearly transgressed.

Hiring an equity educational consultant committed to transforming systems of oppression in education proved to be a singular grace for our school. Late that August, Christina Hale-Elliott and I met initially to talk about our school and to explore the possibility of a partnership. Christina came highly recommended as a consultant among institutions of public education. How would she feel about entering into these conversations with a faith-based institution? Would we be a good fit for each other? I was no longer interested in cosmetic, "one shot," "check the box" approaches to diversity, equity, and inclusion. As I listened to Christina, I felt a strong connection to a shared dream, despite our different life experiences. In the early months of our partnership, I quickly came to appreciate my new location as a mentee.

All my fine intentions to be a "good person" could not free me from my own embeddedness in whiteness and all that comes with being socialized within a racist narrative. Understand, also, that I thought I had already been "doing the work" in this area— as maybe you have thought too. Years ago, when one of my Black students called me out early in a graduate-level ministry course, I heard her, and I did rework my entire syllabus for that course in response to her critique. In class we read Peggy McIntosh's *White Privilege: Unpacking the Invisible Knapsack*, as well as M. Shawn Copeland's devastating analysis of lynching and the Eucharist.[4] It was a beginning. It took me the intervening years of awakening, a pink slip, and George Floyd's murder to realize that I still have a long, long way to go.

Christina's weekly questions exposed my acute ignorance and moved me deeper and deeper into the unseen, unacknowledged, and, yes, unwanted consciousness of my location in unmerited privilege—unmerited because that privilege is mine simply for being white. Her questions pushed me once again into a new and unwelcome "in between." The disempowerment I felt was overwhelming at first. I questioned myself into corners, not sure that any of my ideas could be liberating. I was listening differently to my colleagues, especially my colleagues of color, and as I did, I could see more clearly the chasm between our worlds. Moreover, I could feel that chasm expanding before me. All the bridge-building energies that I had lived as a teacher in inner-city women's schools, encouraging, guiding, and cajoling my students to embrace a brave future, seemed utterly futile in this new moment. My skills dripped of my privilege, my "do for" mentality as opposed to a "be/do with" approach. And I kept running into the missteps of my "do-good self."

I found my prayer turning toward God in the midst of this unanticipated desolation. What I heard there both humbled and encouraged me forward: I realized that I cannot and I *may not* abandon my location in this particular "in between." The approach of real wholeness would not allow me to slip back into the broken narrative. Even as I expressed my personal grappling with this new "in between," telling Christina, for example, that "I have never felt more white in my whole life," she wisely countered, "That is so interesting, Sister Colleen, because for me, I have never not known, all my life, that I am Black." Stay there, Colleen. Stay in the unsettling "in between," I told myself.

Christina and I convened a core working group to initiate our DEI efforts. Both of us were new to the school, and we soon realized that we were facing a rather steep learning curve about the school's culture and its dominant forms of communication. The fact that our presence represented a new administration-led DEI effort exposed fissures among some staff and faculty, who were suspicious of a top-down approach and possibly even jealous of grassroots educational prerogatives that they considered their own. Learning to navigate the mistrust and finding ways into a productive mutuality would take time and patience. It would also take us recognizing that the microaggressions that students and alums were naming were being experienced by some staff and faculty as well.

We proceeded to focus on two important initiatives, even as we realized that there was a significant amount of "prework" to address. A hallmark of our work throughout that school year became a series of focus-group meetings between select constituencies of our school community and Christina. The first such meeting occurred early in the school year with members (faculty and staff) of the school's DEI professional learning community. At that meeting, we learned of a variety of equity and inclusion hopes and concerns: expanding racial diversity; support for LGBTQ+ students, faculty, and staff; the desire for affinity groups throughout our community; the importance of culturally responsive curricula and pedagogy in-service opportunities for a faculty community with significant longevity; and the desire to survey our community members concerning their cultural competence. In the course of that conversation, it became evident that the DEI professional learning community itself lacked clarity about how to communicate DEI growth initiatives to the school administration for action.

If I had had that information earlier in the semester, I might have been able to avert the negative reaction from several faculty and staff members at the opening retreat. Creating a meaningful retreat experience for eighty-plus people on Zoom is never easy. It is particularly demanding during a pandemic. One of the context-setting slides I shared with our community featured a collage of 2020 with a series of comics commenting on our predicament.

Our worlds were literally and figuratively on fire: pandemic raging, racial justice reckoning, political life convulsing, and our western states literally burning up before our eyes. And now our faculty were embarking upon a year of online teaching, a skill to which they had pivoted only six months earlier. It still amazes me that in all that chaos we also embraced the demand to be a different kind of institution. Perhaps precisely that is the gift of chaos: that the moment when everything is turned on its head, the moment when so much ground is disturbed and structures are shaken, is the moment for the new to emerge.

The retreat elicited mixed reactions. Naming our corporate journey at that early moment as a journey toward becoming an antibias, antiracist institution rankled some of our folks. Who was *I* to name this? What resources did *I* bring to the question, and were they trustworthy? What were my antiracist, antibias training and credentials? In this context I had a new and deeper experience of my own white privilege as a barrier to being received as an ally for culture change. It would take the rest of the year and more for Christina and me to build trust for the kind of systemic change we desired.

That fall, our early initiatives included a series of formative experiences. With the support of a core group of administration, faculty, and staff, we outlined a plan of action to address the entire school community. We met weekly to create a framework that would engage faculty, staff, students, parents, alums, administration, and our board of directors. Christina introduced us to the idea of gradually expanding our core group to include and represent all the constituencies of our school community. She also insisted that we be overt and explicit in our response to the criticism we were receiving on social media. It was time for us to make a public statement.

This is what we said:

THINGS ARE NOT AS THEY SHOULD BE

Our world is grappling with multiple assaults on our shared humanity: ongoing systemic racism, COVID-19, political polarization, and natural disasters. More specifically, we acknowledge as a school community that our school has not articulated clearly our response to the historical and social reality of anti-Black racism and other forms of hatred. We know we can

no longer be silent. We can no longer be complicit. Through
social media and direct contact with school leaders, we have
heard our students and alumnae describe their pain at being
dismissed, excluded, unrecognized, and unsupported.

Our community is predicated on the gospel values of love,
compassion, mutual acceptance, and growing into the virtues
of *veritas*, the Latin word for truth. As one of our alumnae
wisely reminded us, "*Veritas* is not a goal, it is a standard." We
acknowledge that we have missed opportunities to live *veritas*
and have not consistently provided our students adequate and
safe spaces to share their experiences of racism and margin-
alization and to find healing. We specifically acknowledge
that we have not adequately assisted our faculty and staff in
responding to the concerns of our Black, Indigenous, people of
color (BIPOC) students and our LGBTQ+ students. We apolo-
gize for our lack of a school-wide response and public acknowledgment to the criticisms raised by our students and alumnae.
Your school hears you, and we are making positive changes.
We want to share what we have begun and what we commit to
create for a future that is true to the standard of *veritas*.

Our statement continued by outlining the concrete steps that
we were taking to address the harms named by our students and
alums. This public act of contrition was only a beginning, but a
much-needed and significant one. The statement itself was the
result of weeks of conversation among the members of our core
group in which we grappled with what to say and how to say it. Our
explicit acknowledgment of our corporate indifference to anti-
Black racism fell hard on the ears of some. We encountered a pro-
tective energy among some of us, a desire to shield the institution
and to minimize the "perceived" harm. However, now as then,
we are continuing to learn that the spiritual experience of facing
our complicity with systemic evil mercifully decenters any false
pretensions of innocence and blamelessness. And as we work to
uncover the spaces where we have failed to see and name the harm

inflicted through the structures of racialized violence, we will invariably recognize and come to embrace the reality of intersecting oppressions wreaking havoc on God's precious children.

"Veritas is not a goal, it is a standard."

We realized we had to go deeper. So, with Christina's wise support, we planned and conducted a public ceremony of contrition and repentance.

VOICES FOR VERITAS
Friday, October 30, 7–8 p.m.

Things are not as they should be.

Many have expressed their pain at being dismissed, excluded, unrecognized, and unsupported.

We seek forgiveness and reconciliation.

We will be hosting a school-wide community virtual gathering to amplify the voices of those who have been hurt and to initiate together a healing journey.

Please save the date for this important event. Registration information to be shared soon.

If you would like to share your story with us, please do so. We want to know and honor your experiences.

Voices for Veritas centered the voices of those who had experienced harm at our school. In what became a liturgy of remorse and recommitment, we held space (online) for our community to gather, pray, listen, lament, and, we hoped, heal.

We started the evening by calling on our God of mercy and reconciliation.

Episode 2

Ever-living, Ever-loving God,

We turn to you this night seeking the light of your truth and the grace of your healing. We are here to acknowledge before you and in the presence of our community the pain and hurt we have caused to your very own children. We want to listen with open and contrite hearts to the brave voices of those who have courageously called us to this moment of repentance. This evening we ask for forgiveness, and we offer our sincere desire for a new and restored relationship with all the members of our school family.

We know that the journey into true communion with each other lies ahead and that this moment is but the first step into your mercy and forgiveness. We count on your guidance as we work to dismantle the systems of inequity and exclusion throughout our school community.

Be with us, stay close to us.

Grounded in our desire to repent, we centered the voices of those we had dismissed in the past. For this event, we invited members of our community to read passages from the Instagram account. In this context we could reframe these words not as attacks on our school, or as the betrayal of disaffected alums, but as the brave voices of our students who believed enough in our mission to call us out and to remind us of our truth. We heard our students and alums name overt transgressions and question obvious omissions:

INSTAGRAM

Where are our educational assemblies on systemic racism and Black history? Where is your recognition of the lives taken by racist police officers? Why is the Black Student Union the only place we talk about Black Lives Matter?

My freshman year, a girl told me that financial aid and scholarship kids were a "problem" and that they were the reason [the
school] was so expensive. I was a financial aid kid. That was the
first of many times I felt alienated on campus because of financial status. That happened the first month I was there.

When I was a student . . . , "lesbian" was the worst insult you
could call a girl. Kept me in the closet way too long. I'd say one
of the hardest parts about being LGBTQ+ . . . is [that] feeling
like being yourself isn't an option.

Boarding students are often treated as props for diversity's
sake. When the cameras are not around, they are treated
terribly, like burdens or sources of comedic material. We all see
it and notice it.

After a contemplative pause, our leaders shared their profound sorrow and contrition for the harm caused. Specifically,
we expressed our grief for failing to protect our students, for
failing to see their unique beauty, and for failing to provide safe
spaces for their flourishing. We grieved our failure to address the
systems of exclusion that pervade both our social world and our
school culture. We grieved our failure to live our mission, to be a
voice of *veritas* in the world.

Then we named the steps we would take to make amends.

First, we would continue to create ways to listen and respond
to the concerns of our students and alums. We identified that
together we were seeking to deepen our understanding of what
needs to change, and to act on that understanding. Then we
shared specific initiatives that we were implementing immediately, including the formation of a new Mission DEI entity, the
Dominican Justice Community (DJC). This group, whose members were to include selected students, parents, faculty, staff,
alums, administrators, and board members, would be trained
to grow their own capacities to promote the work of DEI among
our various constituencies. Their purpose, we explained, is to

initiate, implement, and evaluate our progress toward equitable practices, processes, and systems among our school community. Other initiatives included the continuation of faculty and staff in-service days on diversity, equity, and inclusion throughout the school year; targeted antiracist, antibias in-service sessions with our board of directors, engaging them as stewards of the school's mission and future; learning opportunities for the parent/caregiver community to assure their alignment with the core principles of diversity, equity, and inclusion; regular small focus-group listening sessions to better understand the experiences of our varied constituencies and to plan next steps.

It is hard to underestimate the significance of this event. The feedback from participants—over eighty of them taking part in the evening event—was strongly positive. The sentiment participants most often named was gratitude for the leaders' courage and vulnerability in seeking forgiveness and being willing to rectify injustices.

Reflecting now on those first experiences of publicly addressing our participation in and complicity with policies, procedures, and ways of being that excluded and demeaned, I recall most clearly how the word "repent" fell so hard on our hearts. When Christina suggested that "repent" was, in fact, the best word a faith-based community could claim and embrace, I really had to let the word sink deep into my skin. I anticipated that it would not go over any easier with our leaders, and I was right. We struggled with ourselves, our good and kind white selves, because, of course, we good sisters never intended to cause hurt and harm. Repent? That's pretty serious; and if you attempt to do so without going deep to that place where you see and own your sinfulness before God and your neighbors, then you are clearly not being authentic, not aligning your stated values with your actual behaviors. Since then, our repentance, expressed through our Veritas Circles and all the Mission DEI work we have embraced, has been an expression of our desire to walk in the light of Christ. This light shone on us has elicited both truth and mercy.

As Pope Francis describes mercy, it is the love of God opening a space of devastating divine compassion, rendering us capable of seeing and feeling the broken state of our relationships. Caught in the flow of such mercy, we can be moved to contrition and conversion. Our @dear Instagram account was a *veritas* moment for us, and that moment has had effects far beyond our little school on a hill.

As I continue to reflect on the opening into which we stepped in 2020, naming and claiming our complicity and participation in structural oppression as a school, I visualize us taking initial steps into the flow of divine mercy that has been always, already there, waiting for us. The energies of divine mercy, while at times subtle and compelling, are also tenderly relentless. In the throes of extravagant and searing grace, I see and feel how my attachments and my desires are informed by my "whiteness." This new self-knowledge reconfirms my identity as a sinner in need of mercy and compassion even as I surrender into a new and unpracticed path of self-awareness. This commitment to coming to consciousness about my privilege exposes my judgments of others, my demands for things to go my way, my impatience with interruptions and inconveniences. I experience my "whiteness" in my arrogance and my presumptions. I meet this dimension of myself everywhere: in the car driving in LA traffic, in line at the grocery store with a confused checkout clerk, in our community room discussing some decision to be made. It is always there, that smog of whiteness, and I will spend the rest of my life unlearning and interrupting the neural pathways of white bias.

Yes, I repent of my biases, and daily I go to my core and I pray to be made new by the graces an all-merciful God offers me.

Let's take a contemplative pause and consider what you are taking in as you read.

In another passage from Dr. King's "Letter from Birmingham Jail," he notes that history shows us that privileged groups "seldom give up their privileges voluntarily" and that this is even more so for groups than individuals. "Individuals may see the moral light and voluntarily give up their unjust posture; but, as Reinhold Niebuhr has reminded us, groups are more immoral than individuals."

When have you experienced a moment of communal calling out, as my community did? What happened? How was the situation addressed? What did you learn about yourself? Your community?

How would you deploy the resources of our Christian tradition to address structural oppression and harm within your community? Who would join you? What spiritual supports would you seek to sustain your commitment to justice?

Episode 3

Grounding

"We live out of a deep center of love."

These opening words from our Sisters' 2010 Direction Statement herald our community's shared vision for our future. Grounding ourselves in the deep center of God's love, we seek a "heightened consciousness for relational living." We commit together to a lifestyle that moves out from the deep center of divine love, "building bridges of love" in our world.

In the years since we first wrote those words, our focus on relational living has continued to grow and deepen. We are a small group of Dominican women religious, founded in 1876 by a very young Sister Maria Pia Backes to serve the needs of German immigrants arriving in San Francisco. And here we are now, on the verge of the 150th anniversary of our founding, finding ourselves in a new moment of recognition, a moment when we and our world very much need relational healing.

Dominic de Guzman rooted his preaching mission in relational living when he began the Dominican Order to serve the gospel of truth in the twelfth century. Grounded in a common life of prayer and study, we Dominicans today likewise center our lives in the search for truth and in sharing the good news of Jesus through our works and our lifestyle. Ultimately, this alignment of our words and our deeds—or *how we manifest the mercy of God in our lifestyle*—expresses what Saint Dominic called "the holy preaching," our deeds validating (or betraying) our public preaching.

In what follows, I share the journey on which my sisters and our ministries continue as we work to align our words about relational living with our deeds. I offer the contributions I am making in my role as a theologian and a formator, contributions about what I am learning and how this formative work shapes me. Our journey, both individually and as a community, is becoming our pathway into the transforming energies of authentically living our own Dominican identity: embodying *veritas*. And it is also expanding our horizons, inviting us to recognize and nurture opportunities for mutual formation in our Dominican spirit with our lay colleagues and partners.

And indeed, as both a member of this community and as a theologian, I am finding rich opportunities to bring the gifts of theological education to bear, specifically now on our DEI efforts. Listening to the questions of faith that arise from my sisters and from our ministries' engagement with a wounded world, I recognize a new "in between" for theological education and how my own grounding in theology—the voices and resources I have had the privilege of studying and teaching—might illumine our way forward.

* * *

Grounded in God, we commit to be women of hope and peace in the face of violence. In Christ Jesus, we take a long, loving look at what is real and respond with mercy and justice.

How is it possible to "take a long, loving look at what is real" without first examining how *we* see *others*? My sisters and I are in the process of such an examination. What experiences inform our vision? And how do we construct narratives about what we think we see? We are stepping back and asking ourselves whether our vision was and is clear, and whether our interpretations of what we were and are seeing were and are truthful. Taking such a loving look at both what has been and what is happening now is an integral part of our journey into right relationship as a Dominican community. Stopping and taking stock of our actual practices compel our ongoing commitment to live in right relationship "within, among, and beyond."

Indeed, this *veritas* work beckons us to examine our past and our present. We are learning to do that. And we are beginning to imagine and live more effectively into a Christ-centered future that entails prioritizing precisely such right relationships and practices.

As a community of women religious, we are currently naming how the numerous contemporary calls for justice invite us into more authentic right relationship. For instance, we have only recently begun to learn about the concerns of LGBTQ+ persons. Furthermore, our motherhouse, situated in the rolling hills behind the old California Mission San Jose, was created on land stolen from the Ohlone peoples of northern California. What to do about that? And for the past twenty years we have been exploring racialized perceptions and biases that have unconsciously ordered our relationships as sisters, particularly with our sisters in Mexico.

It takes courage to recognize and address the racism that exists among us. For me, that courage has been an invitation to consider both how I interpret what is right before me and, at the same time, wonder about the persona I am showing (or mirroring) to the world. Do I see myself as others see me? Do I recognize where I need healing and conversation? Am I willing to do the personal work of mending my projections and false assumptions? Such "mirror work"— the internal commitment to see and interrogate the values and experiences that functionally orchestrate our participation in community life—is calling us, my sisters and me, to new experiences of humility and contrition. It is probably calling you, too.

Our community was founded in the late nineteenth century by Maria Pia Backes, an amazing young Dominican woman whose wide-ranging missionary heart pushed her and our young congregation beyond San Francisco to go up and down the West Coast, extending northwest to Oregon and south to Mexico. When I entered our congregation in the mid-1970s, we had a total of thirty-seven schools, six in Mexico and thirty-one in the United States.

This rich missionary legacy is unfortunately also fraught with an offensive history that surfaced publicly and painfully at a major congregational meeting (known as a General Chapter) early in the 2000s. Out of the blue, our sisters from "the region of Mexico" brought to the floor a motion to change our canonical structures, to establish provincial government in Mexico. The initiative stopped our governance committee in its tracks. For all the conversation that had preceded, how was it possible that this idea had not been vetted until now? And beyond the logistics of order, why was the idea such a shock to us? Why our indignation and consternation? A watershed moment in our congregation, our Mexican sisters' request exposed the fact that the communication frameworks we thought had been adequately engaged to finalize our revised constitutions were not truly functional. And it exposed dynamics of both power and privilege that we are still in the process of naming and repenting of, and from which some of us still need to heal. It was a revelatory moment for us all.

Our sisters in Mexico were seeking appropriate autonomy, not separation. Thanks to their request, we US sisters came to acknowledge how our limited engagement and connection had fostered among us an unconscious condescension and a social imagination of "Big Sister, Little Sister." But to say that at that time we experienced a communal calling out of our own structural racism would have been beyond most US sisters' imagination. Even now, many of us are only starting to understand the social consequences of the insidious "colonizing structures" that dominate our social imagination. We continue to be stretched in our commitment to right relationship, being pushed to recognize the ease with which "well-meaning" privileged persons (like many of us) inadvertently foster relationships that reinscribe silence, subordination, and hegemony. We are asking new and better questions of ourselves. We are noticing when opportunities for leadership, knowledge sharing, and joint initiatives across national boundaries present themselves, who has access to these opportunities, and who leads them and how.

From that painfully revelatory moment to the present, our congregational journey has evolved to our current commitment to "right relationship: within, among, and beyond." Our sisters in Mexico have shifted their own language from "discrimination" to "racism" after engaging with recent studies. They have carefully reexamined the province's relationship with indigenous members and with healing the racism they recognize in their own midst. In the United States, as more women of color come to share in our Dominican life, particularly women from Asian cultures, we are asking ourselves, "What does it mean to live well together as an intercultural community?" Our shared journey and desire to be one congregation that responds to the unique social, economic, and ecological challenges of our countries unite us as we embrace common concerns and become "women of hope and peace in the face of violence."[1] We continue on the journey to speak truth to each other and to heal. We continue to be converted. Our focus is on growing in knowledge, care, and pastoral skillfulness so as to be a truly welcoming and inclusive community of gospel women. We desire to live in right relationship with everyone and with our earth.

When I was asked recently to offer our sisters a "definition" of right relationship, this is what I shared and what our community adopted:

> Right relationship is the state of being in which our inner dispositions of mind and heart for wholeness, healing, generosity, and graciousness are in alignment with our actions. Living out of right relationship is a daily commitment of making the gospel of love and reconciliation the center of our being and our doing. As relational beings, we live at multiple levels: personal, communal, societal, and ecological.

For all of us, these intersecting and layered dimensions of our human living all have a role in how we choose "to be" and "to do" in the world. Ultimately it is the alignment between our inner dispositions and our outer behaviors that offers the clearest indication of how our conversion into living for and from "right relationships" is coming along.

There is now a new urgency among us to continue this journey into right relationship, one that Pope Francis noted when he pointed out that the global crisis of COVID-19 unmasked the severity of our fragmented human relationships, "exposing our false securities."[2] He reminded us that these times invite us "to turn our life into a wonderful adventure" and to start to dream together the dream of our common humanity. "How important it is to dream together," he reminds us. "By ourselves, we risk seeing mirages, things that are not there. Dreams, on the other hand are built together."[3]

For my group of Dominican sisters, the journey into *veritas* demands a congregational commitment to a lifetime of "dreaming together," to turning our shared life "into a wonderful adventure." How will we do that? Together, we are taking on a new responsibility for growing in relationship within, among, and beyond ourselves. Within: What needs attention and healing in our individual persons? Among: What reconciliations need to happen between us as sisters? Beyond: How can we bring the gift of our personal healings and communal reconciliations to a world broken by injustice? In short: How will we live *veritas* in our time?

We recognize that this is a formative journey that will ground us in a new way in our deepest values as Dominican women. Concretely, we have adopted a specific way of thinking about how we understand our formational journey. And here is where I recognized an opportunity to contribute from my experiences as theologian-formator preparing students for ministry in our church. I recognized a particular tool's transformative potential if engaged intentionally and over time. Let me share more.

* * *

In our era of GPS, do you ever still look at and navigate by maps? Traveling in Europe with a dear friend many years ago, I eagerly unfolded the guide map to the villages we were hoping to explore. I loved following the outline of the streets that directed our hours of walking, leading us to plazas, museums, and places to enjoy amazing food! My friend was not as excited as I was about discovering new vistas with the help of a map. We had to come to a compromise. Some days we simply set off, without plotting destinations, for the sheer enjoyment of running into a surprise delight. On other days we mapped our journeys. However, even on our undirected days, the map was close at hand because it would, if needed, reorient us.

Early in my work with Catholic health care, I was introduced to a different kind of map. Originally created by Ken Wilbur and creatively adapted by my mentor at the time, Bill Brinkmann, this framework offers a cogent way of thinking about how human persons and communities relate and grow over time. With practice, I came to see this tool as a true treasure map, guiding those who use it astutely with an opportunity to plan and chart personal and communal growth.

For my students in the MA for health-care ministry, this tool became a mainstay of our program. It proved to be a deceptively simple explanatory device for conceptualizing culture change. It also can be a visual and interactive tool for thinking holistically about specific ministry challenges, allowing a leader, or a group of leaders, to employ a values-based approach toward organizing data and thinking together about potential strategies to address complex decisions. From a mission perspective, it can also be a discernment tool or examen for individuals, helping them to consider how their behaviors express their values and commitments.

I brought this treasure map to my sisters. But even before the sisters, I brought the map to our partners in mission. Having seen the model's impact on my students, I wanted to share this tool with the women and men who lead our Mission San Jose (MSJ) schools.

* * *

For the last several years, I have been asked to create formative retreat experiences that engage our educational leaders personally and professionally. Through these annual experiences I have been able to introduce the map to our lay colleagues and invite them to engage in formative conversations together. As sisters, we have a goal to support our lay leaders as they guide our institutional ministries now and in the future. The emergence of lay leadership in our ministries is a direct outcome of the reforms of the Second Vatican Council. Today, our schools are led almost exclusively by laywomen and laymen who have given their lives in service to Catholic education. Many are the product of Catholic schools themselves, and they know the gift that a Catholic education can offer both families and society. The women and men who serve in our schools are highly committed and have a deep connection to our mission. Yet among many of our lay leaders there remains a certain reticence to embrace their roles as *spiritual* leaders of the school communities. A very simple and telling example was the contrast in the content of the weekly school bulletins sent home to parents.

Sister leaders invariably integrated explicit spiritual messages for their parent community. Our lay principals did so rarely, if ever. Going deeper, we discovered an almost inbred deference to the sisters as spiritual leaders, which was functioning as a weird kind of "zero sum" game. Sisters are holy; laity, not so much. Sisters have spiritual training and authority; laity, not so much. Our lay leaders were very adept at telling our mission story, but we realized that we had not yet provided them with the tools for a deep integration of *their spirituality* with our mission. We were all performing our parts but using outdated scripts.

Our lay leaders' continued reliance on sisters to provide the "spiritual voice" of the ministry unwittingly functioned as an abdication of their own unique and sacred spiritual leadership. This is not unusual given our Catholic ecclesial history delineating members' roles. Sixty years after Vatican II, our church

Mapping Right Relationship: The Four Dimensions of Human Experience

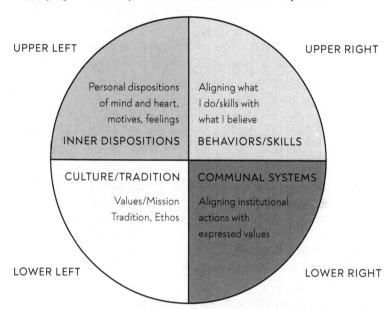

The Right Relationship Map captures overlapping and inter-related dimensions of human experience.

continues to emerge from a dubious legacy that the great Dominican theologian Yves Congar named "hierarchology." Early on, the Roman Catholic Church fell into a "division of labor" that transmuted the early Christian communities' appropriate tension between the church and the world. What the church of the martyrs experienced as a tension between *ekklēsia* and *polis* became, during Christendom, a tension between the "ordained" and the "laity." Over time, and certainly by the advent of the First Vatican Council, the dividing lines of ecclesial labor, so to speak, fell in such a way that the hierarchy became "the church" and the laity, those who "went to the church" to receive the necessary graces for salvation and eternal life. *Hierarchology* describes a deep-seated condition within the culture of Roman Catholicism, which Congar spent his whole life correcting by fostering and promoting the full adult membership of every baptized member of the church.

Unveiling this condition among my lay students in the past and my present lay colleagues continues to evoke spiritual awakenings and connections. Many of these wonderful folks express a deep passion for ministry and a profound love for the mission of the church. They also unfortunately express a kind of "second-class citizen" identity when it comes to trusting their own capacity to articulate the mission that has so genuinely captured their minds and hearts. Given how often I encounter this in my role as a theologian and formation leader, I am grateful for the right relationship mapping tool. Through it, ministry leaders make sense of their experiences—the challenges they face and the faith tradition they are committed to manifesting in the world. So how does the map "work"?

WE EXPERIENCE LIFE INDIVIDUALLY AND COMMUNALLY

We start with the simple and the obvious. We all live our lives as both individuals and as members of communities. Take a moment to let this sink in. While there are vastly different ways in which human communities express both "the individual" and "the collective," across the spectrum of humanity we are "separate instantiations of being" suspended in "webs of relationship" that constitute two distinct and mutually significant dimensions of human life.

How are you an individual? What do you value and cherish about your "one, wild and precious life"?[4] How do you express those values and inner dispositions?

How did you become you? Who are you now? How or what do you imagine yourself becoming?

These are not insignificant questions. Nor are they merely an exercise in self-absorption for the privileged or those with time on their hands. The ability to answer these questions with a sense of inner integrity and life purpose is central to what human communities recognize as the gift of "self-knowledge." And these questions are never answered in a vacuum. The "me" that was, is, and will be is also a work in progress that involves how "I" understand myself in the light of the community that literally and figuratively gives birth to "me." Even, and perhaps most poignantly, in situations of community loss or rejection, that privation marks "me." Relational webs hold us, providing our social, cultural, political, economic, and ecological contexts. From these we draw the raw materials to build a self and to understand how best to live that self in time and space. Communities provide symbolic resources with which individuals name themselves, others, and the dominant values that create order, stave off chaos, and support the collective narratives of "a people."

To whom do you belong? What stories live in you because of that belonging? What does belonging to them mean to you?

Of which communities do you claim the role of "member"? From what traditions, symbols, and forms of life are you consciously drawing as a member of each of those different communities?

What is most attractive to you about your group, your people, your community?

WE EXPERIENCE LIFE INTERNALLY AND EXTERNALLY

If we were to visualize our personal and corporate lives, we would also want to take into account *internal* and *external* dimensions to both persons and communities.

As the figure on page 41 shows, we can map these dimensions of our living as four quadrants. The upper half of the circle represents our individual experiences, both internal (upper left) and external (upper right). The lower half of the circle represents our communal dimension, both internal (lower left) and external (lower right).

The aforementioned Bill Brinkmann introduced me to this way of considering human growth and development and its potential to deepen our consciousness of "how formation happens" in persons and communities. At the time, Bill was a vice president of formation for one of the largest Catholic health-care systems in the United States. His primary role was to work with senior leaders in that health-care system and to provide them with leadership development strongly grounded in theology and spiritual formation. Bill's scholarship and experience prompted him to adapt a model first developed by Ken Wilbur. Bill's own take on the "Wilbur model" transformed my vision as a theologian and helped me to step into and bridge the *between* that often separates spiritual formation and theological education.

At the heart of the right relationship map is the conviction that God meets us in every nook and cranny of our lives. For Bill, the map supported real-life engagement with senior colleagues "on the ground" of their ministry leadership experiences. Where could they "find God" in the daily struggles of leading a ministry that is also a business? Offering selected treasures curated from Christianity's sacred texts, practices, and spirituality, Bill supported the personal transformation of health-care colleagues and tracked the institutional outcomes related to these formative engagements.

One story that remains with me is how a health-care leader returned to her ministry, a senior care home, and started to see things in a new light. She noticed that when patients passed away, the mortuary was called and the body was quietly moved out of the building through a back door. Reflecting on her experience in the light of what she was learning about the dignity of the human person from womb to tomb, she realized that her organization's practice of sending the departed patients out the back door was more like "taking out the trash" than honoring the life of the recently deceased. She changed the way her senior care home released the bodies of departed clients by creating a ritual, inviting staff and residents to line the front hall entrance, singing and praying as the remains were carefully received by the funeral home.

In another instance, two senior leaders, both in finance, became disturbed during a moral theology course when they recognized the extreme gap in compensation between the highest and lowest salaries within their organization. As a result of their engagement with Catholic social teaching on just wages and the dignity of workers, they created and presented to their corporate leaders a plan that would bring salaries in alignment with the justice principles outlined in Catholic social teaching.

There are many such stories that point to the formative effectiveness of good theology—something as simple as offering leaders metaphors from the tradition that immediately signal a Christ-centered leadership style. Think of the impact of a CEO who addresses her senior team for the first time and tells them that their primary work is to "shepherd" this ministry. What expectations does such a simple analogy communicate to a team of leaders?

I remain convinced of the power of the "Wilbur model" and of Bill Brinkmann's interpretation of how to present the model to communities who truly want to participate in personal and communal transformation. I also am grateful for all that I witnessed and learned from my time with Bill and other senior leaders in Catholic health care. Equipped with these experiences, I recognized new spaces where this framework can bear rich fruit. It has been called by different names in the past, but I refer to "the Wilbur model" now as the right relationship map. As I offer my own engagement with the map, I hope you will consider how this map might be of service to you and your communities too. There is no magic about where to begin your reflection on the tool. Below, I begin our deep dive into each of the quadrants with the *upper left* one. Afterward, I will suggest ways to play with the framework as a tool for personal and communal growth.

Upper Left Quadrant

We begin with the heart of the matter, that interior space where the dispositions of our mind and heart reside. Take a moment right now and ask, "What's happening in me right now? Where is my heart?" Pause. Breathe. How do these questions fall on your ears? Do they interest you? Surprise you? Irritate you? One more time, ask: "Where is my heart?" Allow yourself to feel the energy it takes to pause, turn within, and attend to that question. Become conscious of how such stopping to check in on yourself feels in your body, in your spirit. How would you describe what you're feeling? Now, go deeper: What does it feel like to you to step into a space of pause and internal awareness?

My experience teaches me that developing the practice and eventually the skill and habit of contemplative introspection takes time and commitment. Spiritual masters like Benedictine monk David Stendl-Rast and Buddhist monk Matthieu Ricard note that the disposition for internal awareness deepens only with regular, even daily, practice. And while my own lifestyle as a vowed woman religious has afforded me knowledge and formation in the practice of contemplative presence, it is not necessarily "second nature" to people, even those like me who intentionally choose this apostolic lifestyle. We are tutored, mentored, and inspired by the wisdom of women and fellow companions who, by their living, invite us to commit to a daily practice of engaged presence with silence. We work at it.

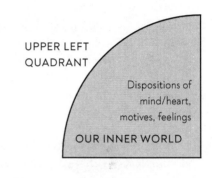

My own journey with contemplative spaces and the practice of presence began early in the process of formation that comes with joining the convent. I really had no idea what "meditation" was about. The best advice I received was to sit in silence for fifteen minutes each day. Fidgety and distracted, I squirmed during those fifteen minutes a day for weeks. Who knew that three five-minute segments could take so long? Sure, I had fleeting moments of an emerging consciousness: "Oh, so this is what resting in 'the quiet' feels like." I found that if I could be outside, in the sun, taking in the beauty of the hills surrounding our novitiate, I was more settled.

Quieting my mind took time and was often frustrating. For me, when I was beset by distractions and was overthinking everything, a breakthrough moment on this early journey to quiet my mind came when I realized that the constant repetition of silently praying the Our Father over and over again filled my head and allowed me to settle into a space of peace and quiet. Many years later, the distractions still visit. "Did I send that email?" "I wonder if..." "Why did that happen?" Just this morning, I was remembering that I had not yet sent my brother his birthday card!

Yes, distractions remain, but I now reframe them as gifts reminding me to return gently to that dedicated space of "no striving" where being present is all that matters. Over the years I've found that attending to my internal life gently opens me to the depths of my being, to my ultimate purpose, and thus to my radical connection to all that is.

Your practice of presence may look nothing like mine. Yours might be a daily walk alone or with a favorite pet. It might be a quiet cup of predawn coffee with a backyard view, or sitting with a smattering of sacred words to help you center. Find your own practice, one that you can sustain, rather than trying to fit someone else's.

Recently, I discovered the spiritual practice of making lists! Marilyn McEntyre wrote a whole book on this spiritual practice, and she notes that making lists can provide us with both insight and personal satisfaction.[5] List making can even open the door to prayer:

> Naming what we want, what we feel, what we're afraid of, naming the uncertainties or delights or questions that come to mind in the moment can help us take stock of our own shifting priorities, our progress or growth in certain areas, and where we need to be re-awakened and pay closer attention to what we have sidelined.

I took her up on her invitation and started to compile lists for my own reflection and growth:

> What gives me joy? Real joy?
> What old hurts are getting in my way?
> What do I really want right now?
> What do I really want for my community?
> What griefs have I yet to unpack?
> What are seven beautiful things I experienced
>   in the past week?

Here's my response to the last list:

1. My ninety-five-and-a-half-year-old mother's pealing laughter
2. White winter light on snow-draped hills
3. Bird song in the trees outside my window
4. The kindness of the Catholic deacon who accompanied my family as we laid a loved one to eternal rest
5. Pinkish-white tulips gracing my writing desk
6. Thick blankets cocooning me in sleep
7. My great-nephew's delight in playing peekaboo

Whatever centering practice we choose, it's our commitment to pause in quiet that opens our hearts to recognize and appreciate the unique spiritual geography of our souls. Psychologically, such a practice makes us more familiar with dimensions of our being that support our personal and social maturation. Such growth in self-knowledge invites us to pay attention to what is happening at our growing edges. Through such improved self-knowledge, through the practice of staying self-aware, we become better at managing how we interact with others. And because our individual lives happen in the context of received traditions and narratives, such self-awareness enables us to recognize the beliefs and values we have perhaps uncritically absorbed as no longer helpful or useful.

All this takes time. Other than a sudden realization, little happens all at once. We all have *internalized biases*. They are an integral component of effective cognitive functioning. Over time, certain associations the brain makes become hardwired and affect and even drive our brain function and knowledge management. So let me ask you, "What do cows drink?" If your first thought was "milk," you have just experienced how bias supports us by managing the data overload entering our brains. The association of "cows" and "milk" has been repeatedly laid down neurologically, such that it is difficult to disassociate the two elements. Thinking for a moment that cows drink milk is funny afterward. Less funny is our association of, say, blackness/Blackness with evil, or whiteness with superiority and goodness, or queer/trans lives with debauchery and sinfulness. Recognizing these and other dehumanizing, even demonizing, biases challenges us to excavate their source and interrogate the social, cultural assumptions that have been ingrained within our psyches and should spur us into accountable change and action.

Related to this challenge is the psychological work of recognizing and working with those dimensions of ourselves that we resist acknowledging or embracing. Each of us struggles with aspects of our personality. What if we reframe them? What if we approached these rejected, repressed, "shadow" features of our person as doorways to greater self-knowledge and personal integration?

Rumi's poem "The Guest House" illuminates this journey with our shadows. At the time I first encountered it, I was feeling self-critical and deeply worried about my employment options. A job I had been offered was rescinded after the institution did some financial recalculating and decided they could not afford the position. Anxiety escalated to self-doubt and the situation was compounded as I struggled with my fear, anxiety, and anger. Rumi's poem seemed so strange to me then. Welcome the unwanted, troubling "guests" of anger and self-pity? Really? I wanted them out! All of them! Now! Only with time and a good spiritual director was I able to begin to relate to the dimensions of my personality that I relegate to the shadows.

I remember a pivotal graced prayer time when in my mind's eye I saw an incomplete circle; it had a big chunk spooned out of it. And in that moment, I realized that I was only willing to come to my God if I could show up without my anger. I could only come to God with that chunk of me, my anger, carved out of me. Hello, Shadow! Yes, I return regularly to David Benner's insight that the shadow is not evil but simply "judged unsuitable and has been denied access to the light of consciousness and the embrace of the rest of the family of self."[6]

The family of self! Yes! And just like any family, the gathering of the clan can and will offer multiple opportunities for interaction and tension. Gathering together "the family of self" is a process that brings into the light of day the inherent tension of holding together all the many members. Instead of hiding and repressing, we acknowledge what is and learn to manage who we are toward a wholesome fullness. For "To deny inner realities is to fail to truly know one's self, and to not know one's self is to risk becoming possessed by that which we have ignored."[7]

Shifting and growing the dispositions of our mind and heart is an ancient admonition that the psalmist knows can be risky business:

> Search me, O God, and know my heart;
> test me and know my thoughts.
> See if there is any hurtful way in me
> and lead me in the way everlasting.
>
> (Ps. 139:23–24 NRSV)

The process of self-knowledge reveals both our light and our shadow, our gifts and our limits, our graced and our wounded being. At the heart of our human journey is the invitation of Spirit to learn how to express ever more freely the truth of our being in the world. It is the invitation to reveal through our actions who we are truly at our core. Attending to the anger I would have ignored or denied in the past is a learning curve that that has taught me both curiosity and reverence for what my anger is seeking to protect me from. Leaning into the lessons my shadows provide continues to ground me as I continue to grow in self-possession.

UPPER RIGHT QUADRANT

If you want to know what I really believe, watch what I do.

Our behaviors reveal who we are and what we value as primary. They are the litmus test for all that we say and profess. There can be quite a rocky road from our actual concrete behaviors to our aspirational self. Learning to recognize the disconnect between our

51

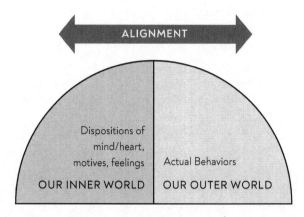

If you want to know what I really believe, watch what I do.

professed values and our actual behavior is an important reflexive practice that is integral to our journey in self-knowledge.

Theologically, this came home to me the first time I read Jon Sobrino's discussion of the difference between orthodoxy and orthopraxis. Sobrino essentially says, "Please don't tell me about the God you say you know and love. I will know the God you truly know and love when I see the idols that you reject and denounce. Show me who your God is by your behaviors. Show me." I remember how I felt when I first read *The Principle of Mercy*, and I have never prayed the creed the same way since then. "I believe in God, the Father Almighty, Creator of Heaven and earth." "Show me, Colleen," I imagine God saying. "How have you aligned your belief in me as the Father Almighty, as the Creator of Heaven and earth, with your behaviors this week?"[8]

Our behaviors communicate. And while it is always tricky to ascribe meaning and intentionality to another person's behaviors, we can and must, for the sake of right relationship with ourselves and others, attend to what our actions communicate. I am learning that this means I must consider more than my intention when interacting with another. I must also pay close attention to my *impact* on that person or situation. I would never intend to harm one of my sisters by teasing her about her food choices, but such teasing can hurt. And the fact that I did not intend harm does not take away the hurt. Paying attention to my impact is a new layer of self-awareness; I learned about it at the same time I learned about restorative justice practices. Before that, I hadn't understood that not intending to hurt does not absolve one from the hurt caused, even unintentionally.

I recently had a painful lesson in owning the harm my actions had on a valued colleague. She bravely told me how my lack of clarity and failure to communicate damaged the relationship of trust we had created. I wrestled with my feelings about that for weeks. At first, I hoped that she would understand that I had been in over my head, and that I would never knowingly hurt her. I soon recognized that I was not owning the impact of my behaviors and that I was looking to her to make me feel better for my mistake.

"If you want to know what I believe, watch what I do." Aligning our dispositions of mind and heart with our behaviors is always a work in progress. And the alignment goes in both directions. Sometimes we find ourselves in situations where the better option is to act our way into a new way of thinking or being. There are times on our journeys when it is in our best interest to "act as if" while we are working through strong feelings or managing a raucous member of the "family of self." Observing and emulating the model behaviors of others offers us a way to a new appreciation and awareness for how to live. Reflecting on our behaviors directs our consciousness back to the inner dispositions of mind and heart. *What just happened in me as I . . . ? What am I learning about myself?*

LOWER LEFT

Thomas Merton wrote: "Tradition is living and active, but . . . does not form us automatically: we have to work to understand it. . . . Tradition really teaches us to live and shows us how to take full responsibility for our own lives."[9]

My curiosity about cultures and traditions goes back to my early days in ministry. Those observations became the seed ground for my dissertation on tradition and discipleship. Living in a local parish community that persons of three major language groups called their spiritual home, I became deeply curious about how culture and religion relate when diverse communities attempt to live together in one sacred space. You can imagine in later years how intrigued I became to work with the "Wilbur model" as a formation tool that made culture one of its pivotal foci.

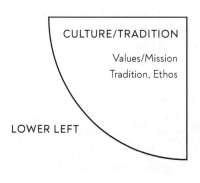

CULTURE/TRADITION

Values/Mission
Tradition, Ethos

LOWER LEFT

I imagine that you have come to your own understandings of the place of culture and context in the art of theological reflection. When I work with this model, I encounter a persistent amnesia (in me and in others) about the deeply formative hold that culture has on both our cognition (or on what we believe is true or real) and our behaviors (how we relate). Our map at this point is particularly important because, in my experience, few of our students or workshop participants have thought about how culture works. My way into this is to tell a story.

I was raised in an Irish Catholic home. I attended public high school because our family could not afford the tuition for private school. At back-to-school night, my tenth-grade history teacher, Mr. Hamilton, made this comment to Mom and Dad. "Well, if there is anything we know about Colleen, it's that she is Irish and she is Catholic!" Dad's response? "You know she did not pick that up off the ground!" Indeed, not! I remember as a small child living back east and walking to the Catholic school we could afford. It was a long walk and, I kid you not, we segregated ourselves. The Catholic schoolkids walked on one side of the street and the public schoolkids on the other. It's just what we did. And at that young and tender age, I remember lifting my heart up to

God in thanksgiving and wonder: "God, how did it happen that I would be
so lucky to be both Irish and Catholic?!"

At a very young age, my sense of belonging to these two distinctive groups had imprinted on my psyche a profound sense of belonging and therefore of identity. The symbols, traditions, and values in which I swam every day gave me a worldview. That worldview helped me construct a sense of self and guided my understandings both of how the world *should* work and of my responsibilities in the light of that guidance. (And, please note, the above emphasis on "should" betrays the role of guilt in my cultural matrix!)

When introducing this portion of the right relationship map, I like to highlight the integral nature of culture to our human development. Going back to my studies, I point out that culture is not something that humans created *after* evolving into Homo sapiens. Culture does not arrive after the fact of emergent humanity. Neuroscience confirms that our earliest ancestors made their evolutionary entrance on the planet only because of the neurological development that foreshadowed the neocortex. This could only be possible by means of some form of sustained symbolic communication that instigated over time the evolution of the layered mammalian cerebral cortex responsible for higher-order brain functions including cognition, sensory perception, special reasoning, and language. As Clifford Geertz points out, culture is not supplemental to what makes humans human. Rather, culture "would seem to be ingredient to those capacities themselves. A cultureless human being would probably turn out to be not an intrinsically talented though unfulfilled ape, but a wholly mindless and consequently unworkable monstrosity."[10]

Yet human cultures, as wellsprings of belonging, are also fallible historical constructions, even though we imbue them with a sense of infallibility and even divine authority. (Remember young Colleen's joyous wonderment of being both Irish and Catholic!) Anthropologist Mary Douglas explains the cosmic consequences associated with trespassing cultural norms. Here's how I understand her approach:

What do folks who "belong" have in common? Douglas would say that they have mutually agreed-upon understandings that constitute their group's shared knowledge base. For example, what do folks who have scaled Mount Everest and survived "know"? Whatever they "know" is also what gives them a unique connection, a social bond, that those of us who have not successfully climbed Mount Everest could not know. When we (you + me) come to agreement about reality (what Douglas calls "constructing sameness"), we have begun to create both knowledge and social bonds. Expand this idea, and we can think of the work of creating social identity as an ongoing project between individuals and their group, in which individuals are tasked with the work of choosing from analogies within the group's tradition and then constructing a coherent "world" from them. Because the world is always changing, our work is to make sure that the knowledges (both received and newly construed) are "up to the task" of managing the ever-changing horizon of human existence.

Consider now how many times our theological worlds have been expanded, challenged, and redirected by emergent knowledges that call out and disrupt received understandings of the good news of Jesus the Christ. I think of the "turn to history" coupled with emergence of evolutionary science, both initially putting the authority of the Bible to the test of intelligibility. When is the disruptive "anomaly" an innovative push of the Spirit, and when is it heresy? For the purposes of the right relationship map, our formative work invites us to listen deeply to the critical questions of our times and then return and take a deep dive into our "repository of knowledges," both Scripture and tradition, to discern what might best serve a wounded world in need of the good news.

Reflecting on how the Christian tradition functions, David Tracy reminds those who seek to live and relate from within this tradition that "there are no innocent traditions."[11] Christianity at its core exhibits a prophetic dynamism for reform and renewal that calls out and denounces any pretensions for power over service.

LOWER RIGHT

James Baldwin stated, "Not everything that is faced can be changed. But nothing can be changed until it is faced."[12]

Want to build a world? Well, consider the worlds you have already built. To me, "seeing" for the first time the webs of relationships that sustain "my world" was simultaneously thrilling and terrifying. The threads that sustain my sense of belonging and well-being are strong and yet tenuous, as are all things of flesh and blood. Not surprisingly, many of my significant relationships are connected to the ministries where I have served and continue to serve. Stepping into the world of a ministry already in process is a little like jumping rope double Dutch—at least that's my experience of entering into a new institutional culture of a particular ministry. There's that initial risky moment of preparing to enter the rhythm of the ropes. We all miss the beat sometimes, and that creates a new opportunity to try again (and withstand spectators' smirks and I-told-you-so's).

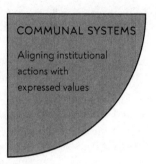

COMMUNAL SYSTEMS

Aligning institutional actions with expressed values

Like institutions, ministries embody cultures. Ministries also exist as webs of relationship, ordered and marked to provide a container in which those who belong can enact their lives and purposes. Ministries, like institutions, have cultural lives of their own and express unique social norms governing relationships through specific policies and practices. Our institutions hold space for what happens between the individual and the group and where the light and the shadow of the whole will have its play.

So the lower right quadrant of the right relationship map holds significant questions for institutions, and particularly for ministries. *Do the stated mission, vision, and values* (lower left quadrant) *align with the actual business of how things are done in the organization? Are the stated public policies, programs, practices, and systems that are meant to animate the life of the institution in alignment with its real culture?* Have you heard the saying "Culture eats policy for lunch"? When I first heard it, I was a little puzzled. Then I had this illuminating experience with a group of senior health-care leaders.

Presented with the stated policies and practices of their organization, senior leaders were asked to grade (A to F) their organization according to how well their ministry expresses its stated mission, vision, and values on paper. The results were very high; almost all gave their institutions an A. Next, senior leaders were asked to grade their organization according to how well the stated values are actualized in the everyday life of their ministry. The results were considerably lower, many in the C and even D range in some areas. This simple exercise showed me just how

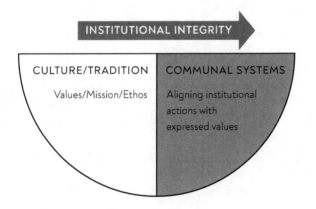

significant a hold culture has on the actualization of a ministry's mission. Truly, culture eats policies for lunch.

How about you? When have you experienced the lack of alignment between your institution's stated values and its actual enactment of its mission? Maybe you have experienced in those moments of disconnect, as I have, the institutional amnesia that seems to take over the push and pull of everyday life. Institutions, like individuals, have shadowed spaces where the failures and the transgressions of the group are hidden—pushed down to subterranean levels where, unseen, they might be forgotten and never mentioned again. Mary Douglas asserts that institutions control the memory of members by diminishing their practice of remembering experiences that take away from group prestige and calling forward group remembrance of events that enhance group prestige.[13] But that is sheer illusion! We have only to look at the Roman Catholic Church's grievous treatment of the victims of clergy sexual assault and abuse to recognize just how disastrously an institutional culture can function, leaving the community morally bankrupted. David Benner's words can easily be applied to institutions: "To deny inner realities is to fail to truly know one's self, and to not know one's self is to risk becoming possessed by that which we have ignored."

ENGAGING THE RIGHT RELATIONSHIP MAP AS A TOOL FOR REFLECTION ON PRACTICE

The more we use a good map, the more we discover. Watching colleagues and students make a conscious connection with the right relationship map is a thrill. The journey of transforming our cultures toward recognizable institutional integrity can only happen if a critical mass of individuals or the significant influencers within a group take on the challenge to seek not simply change but actual transformation.

For me, such regular use of the map as a personal examen continues to be invaluable. I use it to ask myself: How am I actualizing my better self? Such regular use of the right relationship map has even become a form of spiritual practice for me. With its help, I am noticing and paying attention to "what is" with more curiosity and less judgment. And when the judgments arrive, I notice them for what they are. The map supports my ongoing practice toward aligning what I do with my values and personal integrity.

This map can be a great way to engage our communities and ministries with the best of our Christian tradition. Using it can also invite the transformative invitations of the Holy Spirit to meet us in such moments of shared prayer and reflection. Recently, I invited a group of Dominican educators to join me in reflecting on the invitations that Micah 6:8 might hold for us personally and as educators committed to the charism of *veritas*/ Truth. Here is my paraphrase of the passage:

> What is good is known to you, O human:
> act justly, love tenderly and walk humbly with your God.

In the meeting, after dwelling in the Word of God through proclamation and song, we took time to reflect on how God's word expressed in Micah 6:8 wanted to live in our individual hearts. What call were we experiencing? In this moment, what grace were we each being invited to receive as leaders of schools entrusted with the education of young people? Then we considered: How can I respond to grace through my actions? What behaviors might I practice more intentionally for the sake of the community I have been called to lead? Then we took time to share our joys and challenges of school leadership.

Watching our leaders engage in mutual, vulnerable sharing about their lives and ministry affirmed for me the value and gift of working with the right relationship map. Selecting and sharing Scripture from our tradition and helping people make personal connections with their own spirits in the context of their lives here and now felt very much like what Jesus did when he fed the five thousand: I could feel the nourishment being received and shared.

MAPPING GRACE

What changes when we ground ourselves in spiritual exercises like the right relationship map? Maps don't create change: people do. To empower change means empowering people with the tools they need. It means supporting their desire to walk the path of conversion and growth. We cooperate with grace, we wait for grace, and at times we frustrate and refuse grace. Above all, we do not control grace.

The right relationship map might be a way of mapping grace, of tracing the invitations and gifts of prudence, risk, fortitude,

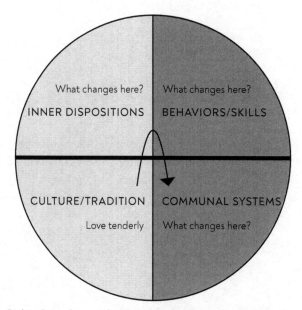

Right relationships can happen when alignment expresses integrity.

and humility that mark us and our communities on our messy and miraculous transformational journeys.

The right relationship map might also be a spiritual direction tool for communities discerning next steps. Scripture, poetry, wisdom from the world's religious traditions, twelve-step wisdom—each of these can offer a point of reflective departure for individuals and groups who seek to embrace the process of moving from "being" to "new being."

Shall we try it? Let's return to Micah 6:8 and see what happens when we "walk the map" and reflect on one of Micah's injunctions, "to love tenderly."

Moving from the lower left to the upper left, we ponder: What changes in the dispositions of our minds and hearts when we take in the words of Micah to love tenderly? When have I loved tenderly? Whom have I loved tenderly, and why? Whom am I refusing to love tenderly, and why? Finally: What needs to change inside me for this encouragement to love tenderly to do its work in me?

Move now to the upper right and ponder: What does loving tenderly look like in my life? What actions of mine have the character of loving tenderly? When was the last time I acted with tender love for another? What behaviors need to change if I am truly to love tenderly?

Consider your community of belonging (or one of your communities of belonging), and ponder: What would it be like if a critical mass of our members were to engage actively in behaviors that expressed Micah's injunction to "love tenderly"? What would our organization look like? How would it feel like to belong to such an organization? What would need to change for our community to be recognized for its ability to love tenderly?

* * *

As a theologian working in between, I have seen the ways the right relationship map can become a powerful tool to share with the multiple communities I serve. As a formative guide and a transformative examen, this framework can be a real treasure map for Christian ministries, charting possible ways of bringing our foundational narratives to bear upon our individual and communal realities. The map invites a dynamic relating with both our tradition and our present historical moment. As a Dominican, I recognize that this is the dynamism that lies at the heart of our preaching and our commitment to *veritas*. In the words of Mary O'Driscoll, OP, "There is nothing worse than a preacher with answers to questions that no one is asking." The interplay of the four pillars of Dominican life, prayer, study, community, and service, can be charted using the right relationship map. Prayer and study ground us into our sacred texts and practices as we engage with the pressing questions of our time. Community becomes the container that holds the workings of the Spirit guiding us to know what might best serve God's people in this moment.

63

You can see that I find in the adapted model of Ken Wilbur a profound resonance with the Dominican vocation for *veritas*. As I have come to know and live it, the Dominican spirit, at its best, is always seeking to enter the "in betweens" of human life: faith and life, grace and nature, spirit and bodies, work and play, contemplation and action. The flow of life over time and space invites us to be wise and careful stewards of the revelatory texts and symbols that welcome all into God's embrace and that are entrusted to us as an ecclesial community. Because the Flesh continues to be made Word, we cannot rest on past articulations of the human mystery when new, compelling evidence presents itself in a changed reality. Equally, our fidelity to the Word that continues to be made Flesh compels us to return to the wellsprings of our tradition. We cannot go often enough to the best of our tradition to drink in the words, the values, the stories, the examples of our ancestors in faith. It is a reservoir for our spirits *if* we choose to go there often and drink. By drinking of the reservoir of our tradition, we are tutored in the practices that express real, concrete justice, love, and humility.

Consider these words from Richard Rohr: "Our knowledge of God is participatory. God refuses to be intellectually 'thought,' and is only known in the passion and pain of it all, when the issues become soul-sized and worthy of us."[14]

My sisters' commitments to live *veritas* by grounding ourselves in a newly articulated understanding of right relationship invites fresh encounters with the Holy Spirit: within, among, and beyond. With those we accompany, we recognize that the mystery of suffering lies at the core of many great human questions. Our Christian faith's response is less a correct answer and more a "walking with" in faith. Our own journeys have confirmed that we are never abandoned on this adventure. In a world where relationships are often "not right," we seek to be a counterwitness for a different kind of world.

Episode 4

Continuing

Restorative justice—a justice that seeks not to punish, but to heal.

—Fania Davis[1]

One of the post-pink-slip gifts of returning to Southern California has been the ability to connect regularly with my mom, who is ninety-plus years young and still living on her own in our family home. In the past several years, remote learning has allowed me to spend stretches of time with Mom, attending to the house and the garden and helping her get to appointments. These are precious and numbered days, a personal "in between" I claim along with my siblings. Our care for our mother is shared differently, according to our unique life circumstances. Work-life balances are never static, and they become ever more poignant in the light of limited time. Walking with my mom in her tenth decade has often caused me to linger a little longer to be present to her. I find it hard to leave her. In a ministry that calls me into deeper proximity with vulnerabilities, my own and others, I find that my sensitive spirit struggles with boundaries. I can overcommit in a misguided sense of responsibility both for family and at work. In those moments, I can find myself in a state that is less creative and more reactive.

On one such occasion I was driving back to school and had arranged a call with Christina to talk about a recent series of interactions among our alum leaders concerning our Mission DEI initiatives.

Reflecting on that call, I remember that I was agitated in my spirit. I was unsettled by the looming tension that was threatening to escalate into relationship-damaging conflict among members of our alum community. Though the @dear Instagram posts had wide support from our alums, several alums shared my initial negative response to the public calling out of our school. And even among those who participated in Voices for Veritas and who supported our engagement with justice initiatives, there was a range of opinions on what constituted real, positive change. Now a conflict was brewing among members of our Alumnae Board, particularly across the generations. I was anxious. I could feel the turmoil in my gut.

So, there I was driving on the freeway, explaining my concerns to Christina. We were still getting to know each other, and, being new to this work, I wanted to get this problem settled. But how? What should be our response? So I asked Christina, "How are we going to deal with disgruntled alums on both ends of the divide? And how do we engage those who share similar experiences but are in very different places about next steps?"

Christina's response? "Sounds like this is an opportunity to consider how we can introduce and grow restorative justice practices. What if we invite the alum leaders to hold space with us and give them the chance to listen to each other and be heard?"

I have a mental snapshot of that moment in my mind's eye, at the junction of the 210 and 605 freeways, because in that moment hope sparked in me. Yes! That's it! That's the way forward!

That personal learning moment is a grace that keeps on giving. And it's a lesson that's not finished with me yet—a lesson in unlearning the sense of responsibility I feel to provide the answers. Maybe as an educator you have been unlearning this too? After fifteen years in secondary education and twenty years in higher education, the practice of providing answers to questions has become deeply ingrained in me. Not that my teaching methods lacked inquiry and dialogue. However, during a semester, there are content goals to meet and, yes, a certain degree of knowledge to engage and impart. What I am grappling with is the expectation I feel as both a sister and a theologian to provide answers, to have it all worked out so that we can get it straight and move on. That's a temptation I have to resist. People may want answers, but primarily what we all need is *a way together. We need to find each other on that way, build our relational capacities, and commit to the journey.* Might this be the fundamental shift in theological education that the in-between spaces of our present time are opening for all of us? We can access all the information the Internet can possibly offer. We can listen to all the news, all the streaming services, all the podcasts, and all the webinars we want. We can be filled to the brim with data. But what we actually need is a way into sustainable relationships. And for our present times, what we need is a container, a space in which we can hold and express our thoughts and our feelings together. What we need is a stretching of our communal capacities through a new and bold attachment to practices of listening, dialogue, and encounter. Pope Francis has written:

> Each one of us is called to be an artisan of peace, by uniting and not dividing, by extinguishing hatred and not holding on to it, by opening paths to dialogue and not by constructing new walls! Let us dialogue and meet one another in order to establish a culture of dialogue in the world, a culture of encounter.[2]

My personal growth in this work is recognizing what is mine to do. One of my biggest challenges in pivoting to this new ministry has been to grow a discerning heart. Our world needs so much healing. There is so much that demands change. Besides that, there is great fear and resistance about doing this work. Our differences and conflicts take an enormous psychic and emotional toll. I am exhausted many days and I know that part of my tiredness comes from my own battle with choosing to trust a way that is both dialogical and uncomfortable. The old temptation to step in, take control, settle the dispute, and move on is never far away on those exhausting days.

That is why this work cannot be done alone. It has to come from the heart and wisdom of a community, however messy and complicated that may be. And *we need to know what we don't know* and have the humility and creativity to seek out gifted partners who compassionately engage with us, even as they hold our feet to the fire.

God sent me just such a partner in Christina.

As we worked out our roles in this mission-centric work, both Christina and I enjoyed leaning into each other's "language games." We had fun in our first months of working together negotiating words and phrases from our respective fields of inquiry! "Tell me again, Sister Colleen, why you think 'mutuality' is a better word than 'inclusion'?" "Christina, what exactly are we doing when we are 'progress monitoring'?" The art of translation became more and more evident to us as we played with how to express important equity educational concepts in a manner that respected the integrity of the concept while simultaneously grounding it in gospel values.

For weeks we worked together and with our core group of leaders to articulate a Dominican educational vision and purpose for the new consultative group we were creating as an expansion of our core group, one representative of each constituency of our

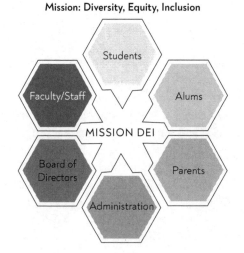

Mission: Diversity, Equity, Inclusion

school community: students, parents, staff, faculty, administration, alums, and board of directors. We call it the Dominican Justice Community (DJC).

As we dreamed and visioned together, we also decided to convene this group only after we had clarified its *raison d'être*, its purpose. Today, the DJC continues to live from this purpose statement:

DOMINICAN JUSTICE COMMUNITY

We convene as a multi-constituency group within the larger community to serve the greater mission of the school: called to faith, integrity, and truth. As a Dominican school guided by the principles of Catholic Social Teaching, we will take systemic, equitable steps to catalyze our emerging future as a safe, brave, and inclusive space, where the dignity of every human is honored.

We embrace the invitation to deepen our understanding of Veritas and commit to:

- growing in personal knowledge and practice of cultural competency, deepening our capacities of inclusion, equity, and diversity;

- initiating, implementing, and monitoring our progress in establishing equitable practices, processes, and systems among all constituents of our community to advance the work of institutionalizing an antiracist, anti-bias school culture; and

- becoming a model community by exercising mutual respect, authenticity, collaboration, and trust.

We purposely designed the DJC membership to center the voices of our school's BIPOC members by a ratio of 60:40. Given the purpose of the DJC, it was instructive and imperative to center the voices of minoritized groups while protecting them from any excessive burden to do the work that is all of ours to do. We also expanded the number of students, since all other members would be beyond their teenaged years.

As a community of reflection, peer engagement, and accountability, the DJC exists to promote and oversee our progress toward becoming ever more practiced in our total school's capacities for diversity, equity, and inclusion. Starting in early 2021, we have met monthly during the school year in two-hour Zoom sessions focused on community building and growing our individual capacities for mission DEI work. With the support of Christina, in those sessions our DJC has explored and discussed the meanings of diversity, equity, and inclusion as a Catholic Dominican school community. Together, we have prayed and paused contemplatively, sharing our faith and our experiences.

We have learned about racism and bias with the help of resources from a variety of justice education providers, including resources from the United States Conference of Catholic Bishops, the Marianist Social Justice Collaborative, and the #BlackCatholic Syllabus. One of my favorite resources is the National Equity Project (NEP).[3] As a theologian committed to unlearning white privilege and apprenticed to the transformational narratives of those who have borne such suffering, I find the NEP collection a formative gift for educational communities following a justice path. Along with other institutions like the National Museum of African American History and Culture, we have immersed ourselves in invaluable articles, videos, and educational materials to support our growing understanding of what diversity, equity, and inclusion can look like on our campus.

These resources were invaluable to us as a DJC charged to refine our definitions and descriptions of what it looks like for our school to be an antibias, antiracist institution. We recognize that we are attempting to correlate these words ("antiracist," "antibias") as gospel values and virtues in a gravely divided political climate. You see, we started this work immediately before one of the more divisive electoral seasons experienced in recent US history, the fall of 2020. Very quickly I learned that even the words "diversity," "equity," and "inclusion" had been politically co-opted. Under the Trump administration, such DEI training, which was intended to educate and equip organizations to be more just and creative work environments, was suspended because, according to the Trump administration, such training wrongly asserts one of two things; either that "the United States is an inherently racist or evil country or . . . that any race or ethnicity is inherently racist or evil."[4]

> *The quality of our relationships with each other will be the clearest indicator to our students that we are worthy of their trust in us.*

Given the political diversity of our community, it remains clear that we must lean into the situation as it is and work to show our community the possibility of naming and living diversity, equity, and inclusion from an authentically Catholic, Dominican perspective. With well-considered, clarified definitions and concrete examples of what *we mean* when we are living diversity, equity, and inclusion as expressed in the life and mission of Jesus, we seek to empower our community to express a new and renewed sense of belonging. And I mean this in the way that Pope Francis intends when he speaks of integral conversion. For our sense of belonging is both a gift and a task. As believers, we know that the Spirit is the author and sustainer of our unity, of our belonging to each other. And that same Holy Spirit is dependent on our willingness to enact the invitations of grace in our time. As I shared with our faculty and staff during a daylong retreat, we can post all the messages we want around the school claiming to be a safe and brave space for our students, but they will believe us and be convinced only when they see us "acting as we speak," or "walking our talk"—that is, enacting goodness, kindness, gentleness, and honesty among ourselves. The quality of our relationships will be the clearest indicator to our students that we are worthy of their trust in us.

Concretely for us as the DJC, we want to attend carefully both to the internal work of individual growth and consciousness (*conversion*, in Christian language) and to the attributes that mark an institution on the journey of becoming antiracist and antibias. Our spiritual transformation as a community invites us to engage with the actual data of what our folks experience as members of our school community. To initiate equitable practices, policies, and systems among us, we will need to "take the temperature of our community" through regular surveys and focus groups, to determine both our strengths and our growing edges. With this commitment to gather and study data, we will be able to reflect, ask better questions, and make prioritized recommendations to our school community for our continued growth.

* * *

One of the goals of the Dominican Justice Community is to *become* a community. This goal is one of the ways that our justice work distinguishes itself as both Catholic and Dominican. Community is one of the four pillars of Dominican life. In fact, our identity as the Order of Preachers (why there is an "OP" after my name) derives not only from our preaching but by *being* "the Holy Preaching" by the quality of our life in community. For Dominicans, our "holy words" are validated by the way we live our lives in charity and reconciliation.

So, I often start my ecclesiology classes with an invitation to consider three words—"committee," "community," and "communion." With what feelings and behaviors do you associate each of the words? Which of these experiences feels the most inviting to you? How would you respond? The kind of culture transformation that living by *veritas* calls for happens only when we can cocreate relational spaces that convince us that "with these folks something amazing can happen." Committees that achieve that kind of connection have morphed into communities. And communities that have the staying power of growing ever-deeper levels of connection mediate that rare and holy condition of communion.

When Christina and I spoke about expanding the core group, I was very clear about what that should mean to newcomers: that our commitment to this justice work must flow from our shared commitment to each other. While we could not impose the intimacy of "communion" upon the DJC, we could name the relational goal: that members of this group commit to being more than merely yet another committee. Adding this expectation was, we knew, a challenge, for most of the members are volunteers with a full roster of commitments outside our school. However, from a theological perspective, the energy for transformation lies precisely in sacred space in which we allow ourselves to be bonded by a passion and a commitment beyond our personal capacities. Such a bond graces our pragmatic efforts with deep faith experiences, and such faith experiences in turn bind us in mutuality and belonging.

Here's what I shared with the DJC at our very first meeting, after asking them to consider the difference they feel between belonging to a community and contributing to a committee.

The decision to name this group a "community" is intentional. It is rooted in our Dominican charism. For Dominicans, we search for the truth TO-GETHER. We live together in community because we recognize that each person contributes to our understanding of truth. Seeking truth and encouraging each other to be transformed by truth fuels our witness to the God we love. In community, the bonds of relationship, lived with compassionate accountability, can be an expression of "right relationship." As a community, we hope that the Dominican Justice Community will become a model of the processes and practices that can take root and bear fruit throughout our larger school community.

Community, in contrast to a committee, provides a container where graced potentials, gestating within and among the members, might find through practices of right relationship the capacities to bring forward more than could have been asked or imagined. Have you had the experience, like me, of recognizing how some of your own gifts and talents emerged because of the hospitality received in a community that saw you and called you forward?

For this reason, our Mission DEI initiatives focus on the single goal of securing this sense of profound belonging among all the members of the school community. "Life is lived on the dance floor between longing and belonging."[5] Spiritual director and psychotherapist David Benner's wise insight highlights the search embedded within every human heart, a search to know and be known, to love and be loved. That quest animates an array of psychic, emotional, and physical drives expressed in the bonds and attachments of our belonging.

Jesus's parables and actions offer us a taste of what the longing and the belonging look like and how those energies disclose who we truly are at our core: beings made for communion. This is a fundamental understanding of the God that Jesus reveals to us—a God whose very being is communion and who calls all created beings into the embrace of divine inclusion. And when our circumstances undermine and prevent us from contributing to such full inclusion and welcome, Jesus's being and doing show us the way.

During one of our recent DJC gatherings, a parent member described the kind of inclusion that I think Jesus is all about. She spoke of being "at the table together" and how, in an inclusive community, each person at the table enjoys a space of belonging and responsibility for all that can happen at that table. We come, each invited by the other, and no one person determines who can and cannot be among us. We come curious and open, willing and able, fully present and owning the space that is ours at the table.

After she spoke, a silence enveloped us. We had all heard *veritas* . . . we had heard the grace she offered us and recognized it for what it was: divine confirmation of our mutual desire for such a table.

For the Christian community, the primary bond of belonging is the "attachment" that the God revealed in Jesus has for each and every human being, and for all of creation. Belonging to the God revealed in Jesus is the quintessential touchstone for every individual Christian and for every Christian community. This belonging to the God revealed in Jesus will always involve a paschal transformation as enacted by Jesus himself in his proclamation and living of the *basileia tou Theou*, the reign of God.

So how do these theological understandings fit into the work that we have inaugurated with Voices for Veritas and the Dominican Justice Community? How do we claim for our Catholic Dominican community the expression of diversity, equity, and inclusion as truly Christian virtues, as "Jesus virtues," to be uplifted, amplified, and practiced? Our advancement team asked me to compose a theological statement to address that question. Here's what I offered.

OUR COMMITMENT TO DIVERSITY, EQUITY, AND INCLUSION

Our students are our mission. We exist to educate young women for a life of faith, integrity, and truth. Compelled by our Dominican charism of *veritas* to seek truth, we act for a just world for the sake of the gospel of Jesus Christ. In particular, as a school sponsored by the Dominican Sisters of Mission San Jose, [our school] is a unique expression of the Sisters' mission to "evangelize, preach, educate, and promote justice and peace."

Our fidelity to our mission calls us to work constantly toward becoming a more just, equitable, diverse, and inclusive school community. Rooted in our Catholic identity, expressed in Catholic Social Teaching, and modeled by Pope Francis, we engage in the worldwide church's mission of promoting *cultures of encounter* by educating and equipping our students for life in a complex, interconnected world.

We value and *choose* diversity, equity, and inclusion because these practices reflect our commitment to create and sustain a vibrant, collaborative, and just community in which the uniqueness of each person is honored as a sacred expression of God's own image, *imago Dei*.

Because the very reality of our God is "Trinity," an eternal mystery of unity in diversity, we claim and choose to grow in our understanding

- of how God delights in the diversity God creates,
- of God's tender care for all as they uniquely express the divine image, and
- of God's hospitality and welcome for all.

We choose diversity . . . and commit to grow our practices of dialogue and restorative relationship building. We recognize that the diversity that delights our God can, at times, trouble and disturb us. Jesus is our model in his practice of healing relationships broken by misunderstanding, distrust, and arrogance. As we learn to listen to the sacred stories of other human beings and practice nonjudgmental hospitality, we contribute to right relationship and express our faith, for: "*That every human being possesses an inalienable dignity is a truth that corresponds to human nature apart from all cultural change*" (Pope Francis).

We choose inclusion . . . in the manner of Jesus and commit to do what he does: "encounter others." Through encounter and dialogue, we expand the circles of belonging that are essential to our full humanity. Encountering our neighbor (often disguised as a stranger) as God's own image, we extend bonds of relationship, recognizing fellow pilgrims who share with us one common humanity. As Catholic Christians we believe that in Jesus, God communicates in a definitive manner God's intention to bring all of creation into a sacred communion of life, reconciling us to each other in order to grow together into one true humanity.

We choose equity . . . as a particular expression of the moral virtue of solidarity, which Pope Francis reminds us is also "a social attitude born of personal conversion [and which] calls for commitment on the part of those responsible for education and formation" (World Day of Peace, 2016). The virtue of solidarity invites us to accompany our students and their families in the enfolding of their lives among us. It calls us to make resources available for our students so that their unique spirits and talents are centered and offered spaces that nurture their growth and maturity, intellectually, spiritually, socially, and physically. The practice of equity, informed by the virtue of solidarity, releases expansive energies for all members of our school community.

As a community, we will continue to define and refine the meanings of diversity, equity, and inclusion for our school. As we do, we want to claim the values that Pope Francis writes about over and over again: We claim the practice of dialogue to foster a sensibility of listening deeply for the truth alive in and among us. We claim a spirit of encounter and hospitable welcome as the means of expanding our practice of inclusion. We claim the virtue of solidarity as a means of leaning into equitable practices, safeguarding the full flourishing of each and every one of our students.

This statement is posted on our website, and, yes, it is still a work in progress. Our DJC and our board of directors continue to reflect on how these words inform more concrete expressions of what diversity, equity, and inclusion look like through a Catholic lens.

My goal is to continue to propose theological statements that spark conversations and give our entire school community a way into the sacred ground from which the seemingly "secular notions" of diversity, equity, and inclusion have their roots. Watching Jesus, we can affirm that diversity, equity, and inclusion are significant, gospel-informed values that repeatedly invite us into *veritas*. When the initiatives for diverse, equitable, and inclusive spaces are understood from this ecclesial, pastoral perspective, Cornel West's words take on compelling meaning: "Justice is what love looks like in public."[6]

May I now invite you into a contemplative pause? Think about this: From the ground of such a basileia ethic, how might we push even deeper and ask:

What does belonging look like in a gospel-animated, antiracist, antibias school community? What are the structures that such a community builds together to support this type of belonging?

What policies and procedures are in place and are regularly evaluated to secure the kind of inclusion that Jesus is all about?

* * *

We knew that so much of our initial work needed to happen with those who interact with our students daily: our teachers and staff. We had a particular responsibility to support them in both their education in the principles that support equity education and in their search for spaces to grow and practice their skills of engagement.

This was also a significant time for me in my role as director of adult formation for mission. One of my first encounters with our school community was as a consultant. On an earlier preemployment visit to the school, I learned that the then-director of mission integration did not feel equipped to host a school-wide conversation on Catholic identity. It was an interesting moment to observe once again that our lay colleagues, for all their desire and even theological degrees, did not feel adequately equipped and empowered to address this question. I volunteered to give that presentation, focusing on both our context and our tradition.

Our context remains one of intense questioning, with a contentious focus on the experiences that constitute identity. There are multiple and various scripts and narratives that seek to address the identity question: "Will the real Roman Catholic please stand up?" Since Vatican II, we have interrogated and found wanting the old markers of cultural Catholicism (i.e., laity are to pray, pay, and obey). Other important human questions like the role of women, family planning, divorce, and remarriage have pushed against long-established and familiar Catholic identity markers. In the fifty-plus years since Vatican II, it is no secret that these questions, unsatisfactorily answered, have contributed to divisions and even a major exodus from our church. I have learned that it is never easy to tamper with people's symbol systems. And that, I think, is what is at the heart of our current ecclesial sojourn. Vatican II proposed in all its sixteen documents a fundamental renewal that decentered the institutional church as the primary way to salvation, and recentered our community on following Christ "in the messianic and eschatological *way of living* in community received from the Lord, until he comes again."[7] This shift to a more biblical, sacramental, and pastorally engaged ecclesial community interrupts past narratives of a triumphant and hierarchically constrained faith community and invites all the baptized to a renewed adult faith, empowered by a sacramental imagination that sustains our capacities for living with and through life's ambiguities and struggles.

Wanting to find a way that would resonate with the school's faculty and staff, I invited them to approach the question of Catholic identity from the "ten thousand foot" level. Here's the gist of what we talked about:

> *Catholic identity is first and foremost an identity found in*
> *Jesus and his way of life . . .*
> *. . . a way of life that had dire consequences,*
> *resulting in a community of faith*
> *radically transformed by their encounter with*
> *Jesus Risen.*
> *Christian narratives witness to and reveal*
> *a God whose living Spirit animates*
> *the evolving mystery of creation*
> *caught up in Self-Bestowing LOVE.*

We paused just to be with that "view from ten thousand feet" of the Christian mystery. It was important for me to highlight that Catholic identity emerges from a living tradition fundamentally animated by the Spirit who secures the tradition's capacities to remain dynamic and open, not static or closed. Yes, it is undoubtedly true that our Christian communities have a checkered history. We are not innocent of the sins of the past two thousand years. And it is equally true that we are easily seduced by sin and taken in by false personal narratives of moral rectitude and righteousness. As David Benner writes,

> It is quite astounding how easily an egocentric, willful life can survive the cultivation of "Christian" virtues and spiritual practice. The best marker of this is investment in maintaining control. A second close sign is the extent to which life is lived with resolve rather than release and consent.[8]

I return regularly to these words of David Benner. I recognize in myself how the desire to control outcomes, to have the answers, narrows my capacities for dialogue and genuine curiosity about the experiences and thoughts of others. I don't think I am alone in this. So, when I asked the group to reflect gently and nonjudgmentally on their own moments of exaggerated control, the room fell silent. Then I asked them to consider a moment when they allowed a situation to unfold on its own, when they received reality with "release and consent." Again, a deep silence. I understand this kind of silence as graced quiet when we have touched the soul of the group and we are walking together on sacred ground. Benner's words ask us Christians to consider how we are integrating the deepest truths of our faith tradition, how that "traditioning" is showing up in our behaviors. Since every religious tradition dwells in ambiguity, it takes attending to that tradition to discover the elements that will animate the best of our humanity.

Take a moment to reflect on Benner's words for yourself. Here they are again:

> *It is quite astounding how easily an egocentric, willful life can survive the cultivation of "Christian" virtues and spiritual practice. The best marker of this is investment in maintaining control. A second close sign is the extent to which life is lived with resolve rather than release and consent.*[9]

Consider the life conditions that elicit a constricting and controlling response from you. What do you notice?

When have you been able to live life with release and consent? What does that feel like in your body?

What would change for you if you invested in behaviors of release and consent on a regular basis?

CATHOLIC WORLDVIEW

Dignity of the Person and the Common Good
Analogical Imagination
Open to Mystery in an Evolving, Unfinished Universe
Respect for Reason
Sacramental Vision of Reality

Moving from that ten-thousand-foot level to a more grounded vision of Catholic life, I suggested the above five interrelated dimensions that mark a Catholic worldview. Each of these aspects invites and supports our relationship with the mystery of God revealed in Jesus. And each has a role in our identity as a Catholic Dominican school. Our Catholic Christian faith affirms that the God of Jesus is One who moves toward us first, seeking us out, in time and space, for relationship (Dignity of the Person). We can trust this God, and we can trust our limited human capacities to "know" this God if we remain open to the mystery of God already present in our present (Analogical Imagination/Sacramental Vision). Our trust is not an arrogant assertion of our exclusive take on the divine mystery or human life. Our reason remains limited, and creation "unfinished" continues to evolve (Respect for Reason/Evolving Creation). We need each other and each other's perspectives in order to know and love this God truly. Hence, our journey into *veritas* compels us to search humbly and together for the truth, acknowledging our profound need for each other's experiences, insights, and questions (Common Good). As a Dominican school, we are animated by the desire to know and serve the Truth. Our eight-hundred-year tradition as Dominicans affirms that *veritas* happens in communities of dialogue, communities that are respectfully curious of the diversity of experiences we might not comprehend easily given the limits of our cultural and social locations. In the words of Bishop Pierre Claverie, "There certainly are objective truths, but they exceed our grasp and can be attained only through the long journey which we piece together by gleaning from the different cultures and instances of humanity what others have sought and obtained in their own journey toward the truth."[10]

I am reminded of the right relationship map (see Episode 3). Digging around in the Catholic Dominican tradition (lower right quadrant), as a theologian, I culled treasures from our faith tradition to share with these faculty and staff members to support their mission engagement within this ministry. The pastoral question that follows theological discourse is "What changes now?" Engaging with key, life-affirming elements of Catholic identity, what difference will we work to create together? This question engages our personal behaviors (upper right) and could affect our school's climate for the good (lower right). I offered these concrete suggestions for our school community's consideration as a way forward together.

- Protect the human dignity of those with whom I disagree.

- Protect my human dignity with clear, nondefensive points of view.

- Recognize how "fundamentalism" might be functioning in me and others. Work on me first.

- Stay curious, stay courageous.

- Allow questions to have the time they need to gestate. Love the questions!

- Own my feelings and find safe places to speak my mind respectfully.

Reviewing these suggested practices now, I am struck by how they foreshadowed the work that would be mine in 2020. Fast-forward two years from that retreat morning, and our world would contract even more. For our faculty, the personal and professional burdens of adjusting to a worldwide pandemic and pivoting into new ways of delivering excellent online educational experiences were taking their toll. If we were going to succeed in offering meaningful DEI in-service experiences that would have a positive effect on students' experiences in the classroom and among us as colleagues, we would need to continue to foster dialogical practices that would help all of us to "stay curious, [and] stay courageous."

Embedding dialogical practices takes both time and intention. I continue to notice and be repelled by "one shot," "quick fix" approaches to the justice work of diversity, equity, and inclusion. Before we could begin to consider definitions of diversity, equity, and inclusion or our experiences of microaggressions and bias with our school community, we had to model and rehearse the type of restorative conversations that would promote right relationships among us. That is why the practice of returning to agreed-upon "norms of conversation" introduced to our school community during our very first workshop with Christina has become a mainstay for me, personally and professionally.

- Use "I" statements.
- Listen to understand, not to respond.
- Own your intention and your impact.
- Approach conflict constructively.
- Be mindful of your participation.
- Expect mistakes, discomfort, and lack of closure.
- Maintain the privacy of others who share.[11]

Christina developed and refined these seven behaviors over many years of equity educational consulting. You might recognize some of these norms from your own work with restorative practice circles. While at times our community adapts the original norms (depending on the meeting or our goals), I continue to find these intentions to be a powerful way to remain conscious of the dispositions of mind and heart that promote inclusion and respect for all participants. Sharing specific "norms for conversation" and offering concrete examples for each one actually offered us more than guidelines for conversations. The intentional practice of these strategies can offer a way into spiritual practices that centers the humanity of others and raises communal consciousness for attending to right relationship. This is exactly what I learned when I offered these very same practices to our sisters as concrete ways of expressing restorative right relationship. When adopted and enacted intentionally, these norms become forms of spiritual exercises and best practices that promote healthy relationships and personal integrity.

Here is a way, not an answer. Here is a small but powerful way to take personal responsibility for the quality of my relationships at home and at the office. A gift of indigenous wisdom that holds all life with respect and dignity, even those that harm us, these restorative practices help us to become better at living the dynamic between the individual and the communal. Even as I continue to be challenged and even provoked by those who think differently and who resist our commitment to becoming antiracist and antibias, I also recognize my own arrogant ego and my attachments to inner fundamentalisms, and I continue to learn the lessons of how to be curious, courageous, and accountable.

In what follows, I share my reflections on practice drawn from my engagement, including my challenges, with each of the practices. Just as a single pebble creates ripples that extend beyond the first point of contact, these "norms of conversation" first shared with our faculty and staff at an in-service session have since been shared with our board of directors, our alums, and our parents. Most significantly for me by far has been the impact of sharing these norms as spiritual practices with my sisters. Little did I know in that first sharing that my community of sisters would intentionally adopt these practices or intentions as concrete ways for living our lives together in right relationship. I knew this work was bearing fruit beyond what I had imagined when I heard, months later, the preaching of one of my sisters and her moving personal reflection on how she has been integrating the practices as part of her journey into right relationship.

This list is not exhaustive. What would you add? What wisdom do you practice in service of right relationship that might complement what you find below?

Use "I" statements. Speak from your point of view and experience. Take responsibility for your experience and honor your perspective. Dare to trust your voice and pay attention to the times when you make assumptions and attempt to speak from the "you" narrative of someone else instead of an "I" narrative that belongs solely to you.

Listen to understand, not to respond. Real listening is a fine art in which we make interior space for the voices of others. This discipline requires that we attend both to what we hear and how we are taking in what we hear. We are often not able to listen deeply because we have been triggered and are already "talking back" in our heads. Our listening space shrinks, and we miss the full communication of the other as our internal banter awaits the moment the other person stops so that we can start. When we listen to understand, we preserve an internal space of curiosity, interest, and openness to the unique voice we are experiencing. A sign that we are not really listening is the propensity to interject quickly "our version" of the other's experience. "Oh, when that happened to me . . ." Watch for the ways in which the temptation to become immediately self-referential shuts down the conversation's potential to be about the other person.

Own your intention and your impact. Taking responsibility for both our intention and our impact is a particularly demanding restorative practice. While it can be very clear that we did not intend a certain outcome, if we are the source of that outcome, we have a responsibility to own the consequences that our actions or inactions had on a situation. I never truly integrated the difference between intention and impact until Christina shared a story. She recounts a time when she and her older sister were running to get into the family car. Her sister arrived at the car first and was unaware of her little sister running right behind her. She closed the car door just as the little hand reached to get in the car. Big sister immediately ran to get Mom and Dad and to find ice for the injured hand. Big sister did not say, "I did not see you. Stop crying, I did not mean to hurt you." Because she instead *attended* to the hurt, she was already indicting that she did not *intend* the harm. Attending to the harm caused is the way we express our intention that it did not happen. A response that only expresses what I did not intend ultimately expresses a defensive and dismissive posture toward the other person.

Approach conflict constructively. For many of us, conflict becomes almost immediately a negative, adversarial experience. The tension that is created, if not dealt with creatively, will easily devolve into power plays resulting in defensive positioning at best and demonizing dismissal at worst. While it is important to stand by our ideas and ideals, it is also important to hold them with a "relaxed grasp," particularly when challenged by another perspective or life experience. Conflict, embraced as part of a human learning curve, can support the emergence of an intentional community of uniquely gifted and mission-empowered individuals who allow the push and pull of perspectives to hone outcomes that could not emerge without the conflict. Approaching conflict constructively requires a confidence in the process of engaged interaction with different ideas and perspectives. This practice is particularly demanding in terms of emotional intelligence and maintaining a disciplined check on the ego. Among all the practices mentioned here, apprenticing to this practice holds the most potential for a truly humane future.

Be mindful of your participation. Consciousness is everything! Take a breath and assess your "internal weather" as you interact in the group. Attend to your body. Where are you feeling tension? How are you breathing? How is your heart rate? Coming to body consciousness and attending to feelings while participating in a group can help you maintain your center and stem possible emotional reactivity that might be triggered. Breathe, and if you find yourself triggered, continue to attend to your breathing. The 4-7-8 breathing practice, developed by Dr. Andrew Weil, is a helpful natural tranquilizer for the nervous system and can help to assuage internal tension.[12] From a place of mindfulness we are then able to assess the appropriateness of our participation and avoid both overtalking and undertalking. Attending to our cultural conditioning while participating in a group endeavor is also key to productive group outcomes. Given our particular cultural frameworks, we may be challenged to resist learned passivity or the inclination to take over the activity.

Expect mistakes, discomfort, and lack of closure. This practice invites us to create a gracious space for human error even as we hold ourselves and others compassionately accountable. One of the maxims of DEI work is the intentional cultivation of the capacity to become comfortable with discomfort. The inherent paradox of this practice grows our capacity to stretch into spaces that represent our next growing edge. Resisting discomfort, emotionally and intellectually, limits our growth potential and results in less creativity and flexibility in an increasingly complex and changing world. Recognizing the difference between the capacity to hold a lack of closure and outright indecision is itself a process of discernment that, refined over time, marks a highly skilled community member. As best as I can imagine, there is a confidence that animates the capacity to hold the lack of closure represented in a gestating question or experience. This confidence recognizes the harm that a rush to judgment can inflict by sabotaging due process and more. On the other hand, fear-imbued avoidance seems to accompany indecision, the conundrum where not deciding is in fact a decision.

Maintain the privacy of others who share. Confidentiality is a gift we give to others, honoring the unique humanity and vulnerable journey of each person. Since each of us is a work in progress, the commitment we make to secure the safety of another's unfolding life story and learning redounds to our own well-being. In that safe space we can explore our questions and wonderings without fear of gossip, misinterpretation, or retribution.

* * *

Initiated with faculty and staff, and now recognized and regularly practiced by my Dominican sisters, these norms of conversation exemplify concrete restorative practice behaviors and are a mainstay in our Mission DEI work. Whether working with the board of directors, alums, or parents, reviewing these norms at the beginning of significant processes encourages participants to foster a climate of dialogue, encounter, and inclusion. We are learning how to lean into diverse perspectives and how to ask questions, while remaining true to our own experience without negating another person's reality. As Christina reminded me, "Sister Colleen, two seemingly opposite things can be true at the same time." Growing all our capacities for this kind of diversity, equity, and inclusion remains our ongoing gospel challenge and privilege.

Episode 5

Amplifying

Jesus reveals to me the infinite value of every human being, precious in the eyes of God. He allows me to recognize in the other the call to get out of my limits and my dominating arrogance to discover in him what I still lack to be fully, authentically, generously human.

—Pierre Claverie, OP[1]

In bringing theology to bear on communities who want to dismantle racist and biased systems, I am discovering that the energies of supremacy, dominance, and exclusion cut across multiple marginalized communities. The amplified voices of those who courageously name such injustices draw me down into layers of their pain, hurt, and suffering. Fania Davis, social activist and healer, helped me a great deal in this way by describing her own journey of resisting injustice and her own experience of intersectionality.[2] Deploying the metaphor of a car accident, Davis exposes and amplifies the layers of harm and hurt that converge on persons who hold in their being multiple minoritized identities. In Davis's example, a woman of color who also identifies as queer is harmed. When the metaphorical emergency caregivers arrive, which harmed identity will they prioritize? Being a woman? Being BIPOC? Being LGBTQ+? Such is the predicament of addressing intersecting oppressions. Structural harm is happening to this one human on all three levels of identity. The experience of such harm is catastrophic for her. Where to begin healing? Whom to trust? Is healing even possible in a world controlled by dominant and resistant social identities that will not make space for others like her?

Recognizing such intersectionality is important because mechanisms of exclusion function in a similar manner. And there is a cruel "made-to-be-invisible" history that these "othering" social functions inflict on those they deem unworthy of notice or care.

As a community of Dominican sisters, we discovered our complicity with this kind of harm in the @dear Instagram posts received from our school's LGBTQ+ alums and students in 2020.

INSTAGRAM

I'd say one of the hardest parts about being LGBTQ+ on the hill is [that] feeling like being yourself isn't an option.

How was it that we were not seeing or responding to our LGBTQ+ students? Clearly we were seeing some of them. We knew of those few students who came to feel loved personally and who trusted that they could share who they are with one or two of us sisters. Often, their stories were about how to tell their parents (or not). "Please, Sister, don't let my mom and dad know that I am participating in this support group. They would kick me out of the house." Sadly, we all know that such parental and familial rejection is not unfamiliar to LGBTQ+ children. Toxic ideas and projections of "not normal" are part of the system of shame, rejection, and violence that many of us have perpetrated on the queer community for years and years. As one of our students recently asked me, "Sister, why do people focus on sexualizing us? Why can't people just see that we are just as human as they are?" I still see the pathos in her eyes, holding that question. I heard her question a little more pointedly. She may or may not have intended this, but given the context of a Catholic school student asking a religious sister this question, I understood her to be asking: "Sister, why is it that your church and this school see my queer identity as exotic, weird, and morally questionable? Why can't you see me as just another kid with a whole host of identities that are part of who I am becoming? Why can't you love me for that?"

In Leonard Cohen's words: "There is a crack, a crack in everything. That is how the light gets in."

I am where I am today because of a personal *veritas* journey—my journey of truth—that exposed my own complicity in ecclesial systems of bias and harm against LGBTQ+ persons. For all these years, I have known and yet still decided to continue living with the ambiguity of my Catholic tradition. Why? Because despite the inherent hierarchical sexism and fear of the gifts and powers of women, daily I meet Jesus here, in this wounded ecclesial tradition, and with him I choose to stay. I have received amazing gifts from this often-difficult community. One of these gifts is the grace of embracing with Jesus the cruciform character of divine love: a way of being and doing that chooses to love from within broken, incomplete, and even unloving situations, fueling those inner transformations only fully known in the mysterious heart of the divine purposes. So, in the past several years, I have been asking myself about my fear concerning how to speak to and support LGBTQ+ persons in our church.

My first step: to examine my own bias about and toward LGBTQ+ persons. I wanted to think that I didn't and don't carry that bias. However, I discovered that I do. Those deeply internalized prejudices have made me afraid about how to be both Catholic and a welcoming ally to LGBTQ+ persons.

Writing this seems a bit strange to me because "some of my best friends are gay." And I have enjoyed close friendships that remain mutual and loving. You, too? I realized that most of my good friends in the LGBTQ+ community are not activists. Interestingly, they are all ministering in one way or another in the church and manage to do so keeping a low profile. One of my dearest friends used to gather regularly with a small group of gay Catholic men, presiding over Eucharist and ministering other sacraments. He shared with me years ago that he was able to do this only because he kept quiet about it, and he wondered whether he would be asked to stop this outreach should he be made chair of his theology department.

Stories like these have been my overriding experience. Either my gay and lesbian friends and students leave their ministry or our church and find a new welcoming home in other Christian denominations, or they stay undetected, living in "stealth" mode within our ecclesial home.

Four years ago, this all started to change for me when I began to work regularly with a group of our Mission San Jose Dominican educational leaders. Working with these amazing leaders and following the thread of educational challenges they were facing on the front lines of their schools became a catalyst for my own growth and conversion from fear.

It all started when the sister in charge of our sponsored schools asked me to give a two-day retreat for the leaders of our Mission San Jose schools. I began by introducing them to the formation process I had been practicing with ministry leaders in Catholic health care. (See the right relationship map in Episode 3.) Specifically, our goal with this group of Dominican educators was to deepen their engagement and their ownership of our charism. We sisters embraced this amazing opportunity, recognizing that we were actively "midwifing" a new vision of church and school ministry among ourselves and our lay leaders. Our goal was to empower and animate our lay leaders to take a serious and deep personal dive into their inner lives/dispositions and to bring the treasures of their own spirituality and wisdom to the surface, to make their unique light shine for our shared mission. My previous work with health-care leaders taught me that when people connect their spirits and unique spiritual gifts with their work, something powerful happens to both the leaders and the organizations they shepherd.

While our lay principals are excellent educators and administrators, we sisters were reading "the signs of the times" and could detect a vital missing piece: personal formation in the Dominican charism *as a community leader*, that is, providing the conditions for our leaders to connect their distinctive spirits to our shared mission. Our sisters' leadership team invited me to create experiences that would help these educators grow and deepen that very connection between their own spirits and our charism. What a privilege!

So, we just might ask: What is "spirituality" anyway?

As I have done with retreat participants, I invite you to step into an experience with me and try this. Right now, in the space below, draw a person that you think is a "spiritual person." What are they wearing? In what behaviors are they engaging?

My idea of what a spiritual person looks like

Now take a moment and visualize a person who "has spirit." Go ahead and draw that image below.

My idea of what a person who "has spirit" looks like

What are you noticing about your two drawings? Take a moment to ponder this. You see, if I simply ask people to tell me about their "spirituality," the room often falls silent. For many of us approach the idea of spirituality from a false notion that only a few special, esoteric people are "spiritual." Doing this simple exercise consistently produces "aha moments" and contributes to a wonderful new curiosity about what makes our spirits "come alive." [3]

Back to our educator-leaders. After a day of exercises like the one outlined above, and after exploring the upper two quadrants of the right relationship map, we began to explore the social challenges that were calling for our best engagement with reality, specifically as it was presenting in our school and parish communities (the lower two quadrants). Our conversations were animated and collegial. They quickly made clear that our next annual conference needed to include time to explore how to attend creatively and faithfully to three major social movements: racism, anti-immigration, and LGBTQ+ concerns. These three social concerns were showing up in all our school communities, and our lay leaders were grateful to have discovered that they were not alone in addressing these realities with their people. We could work together and support each other with ideas, strategies, and a shared moral commitment to express the gospel of Jesus within our Dominican schools. As a facilitator and theologian, I could work with confidence on the first two of these social movements: racism and immigration. The third—LGBTQ+ concerns—was a new horizon to me in terms of both knowledge and my conversion.

I can recall where I was when I got in touch viscerally with my fear and hesitation about this: I was sitting at my dining room table in St. Louis, the plan for the next two-day retreat conference emerging. How might we take the next step toward integrating a spirituality of leadership in the Dominican tradition while addressing current social justice movements in the spirit of our charism?

The theme for the two days grew out of this dual goal: "Missionary Discipleship: Doing the Truth with Love at the Margins." I knew from working with some of our school communities that addressing racism and immigration during a contentious political season would be a tall order, but also that it would not be enough. We needed to address the experiences of our LGBTQ+ Catholics if I was to be faithful to the promptings of the Spirit among us. And at the same time, I could feel myself shutting down and wondering, *How will I be able to represent the church* and *the teachings of*

the church in a manner that will both be faithful and not cause harm?
I realized in that moment that relying only on my own resources
was foolish. I reached out to a colleague and asked him to be a
thought partner with me, and to be a sounding board for the fear
and anxiety I was feeling. It was comforting and strengthening to
learn that this was a topic dear to him; he had journeyed with his
own brother whom he had loved and supported as a gay man.

I soon discovered that my fear and anxiety largely derived from
my (mis)perception that there might not be an authentic Catholic
way to support LGBTQ+ persons on their journeys. So, in fidelity
to the Dominican charism that lives in me, I started to study. My
colleague and I committed to reading more of Fr. James Martin,
and particularly to reading and discussing Martin's *Building a
Bridge*.[4] As I read Martin's text, the depth of my ignorance began
to dawn on me: I had never interrogated my bias about "the gay
community." Having lived for several years just blocks from the
Castro in San Francisco, my bias was informed by a perception of
"the gay lifestyle," which I experienced as aggressively sexualized
and exotic. At that time in my life, no one I loved participated in
Pride parades or claimed allegiance to the overt gender expression politics that dominated my years in San Francisco.

Martin's text changed me. I found myself listening to him as if
he were in the chair next to me. Through his writing I heard him
say, "the work of the Gospel cannot be accomplished if one part
of the church is essentially separated from any other part."[5] I felt
his love for the church, for all the people of God, aligning with
my own love for the church. He helped me to see the stunningly
simple affirmation that, for Christians, our first identity is our
baptismal identity: we are all God's beloved, named such just as
Jesus himself was at his baptism.

As Martin amplified the voices of queer Catholics, my misper-
ceptions and anxieties were coming to light. Of what am I really
afraid? What is this block that I feel when I think about speaking
with "respect, compassion, and sensitivity" about queer folks?[6]
Isn't that what Jesus asks of all of us in his community? The cen-
sure of some conservative bishops and the silence of most bishops

contributed to my dilemma. Having lived with past draconian diocesan oversight of schools around LGBTQ+ concerns, for instance, refusing to allow gay-straight alliance organizations on campuses, I (and others of my colleagues) internalized a very real threat coming from our local church leaders that public support of LGBTQ+ youth in our school places us outside of our Catholic identity. There it is. The deepest lie: You cannot be queer and Catholic. That's what is really at stake here. This struggle between the institutional church and LGBTQ+ Catholics is an ecclesial conflict that belongs to all of us. That is what Martin taught me.

Reading Martin's text fueled my desire to study and to grow a new imagination about gender and sexuality. In many ways, that moment was an experience of multiple streams of reflection and questioning coming together such that my thinking was literally "reorganized." My new question became: *"Why are we not protecting God's precious people from the viciousness of anti-LGBTQ+ hatred?"* Furthermore: *"How can we stand by and ignore what we are inflicting through our complicity and our silence?"* I knew I could not continue on the old path.

And then the floodgate of resources started to open. The Marianist Social Justice Collaborative's guide for educators sealed the deal in my heart as I took in the statistics:[7]

> LGBT students are more than 3 times as likely as straight students to say they do not feel safe at school.

> About 3 in 10 LGBT youth have attempted suicide. Besides, LGBT youth are up to 3 times more likely to attempt suicide than their heterosexual counterparts.

> A 2009 survey of more than 7,000 LGBT students aged between 13 and 21 found that in the past year, because of their sexual orientation:
>
> · 8 of 10 had been verbally harassed at school
> · 4 of 10 had been physically harassed at school

- 6 of 10 felt unsafe at school
- 2 of 10 had been the victim of a physical assault at school

These data confirm what my LGBTQ+ colleagues and students have shared with me about how their very existence is literally under threat. And I have experienced firsthand the resistance and visceral anger provoked in some when sharing these data concerning LGBTQ+ youth. There is among us a long-reinforced reticence—no, a refusal—to accept the reality of queer Catholics in our church. On reflection, it eerily parallels the Catholic refusal to warmly, genuinely, and fully welcome Black Catholics in our church.

Now I was ready. Recognizing a new responsibility to amplify the voices of LGBTQ+ Catholics, I decided to center our retreat with our Dominican educational leaders in our charism, *veritas*, and to explore together how the Spirit of truth both invites us and empowers us to respond to those threatened by oppression and hatred.

It was a powerful two days. We set the foundation for our conversations about racism, anti-LGBTQ+ bias, and anti-immigration in the context of our Dominican vision that looks at the world and asks, *"Where is the spark of the Spirit calling us to pay attention?"* With the help of the insights of Edward Schillebeeckx and Johann Baptist Metz, we grounded ourselves in the skills that would help us to listen to and amplify the "cross grain stories" of our times: those stories that literally "cut against the grain" of the dominant narratives structuring our relationships and calling them into question. Grounding ourselves in the tradition, we pondered how these stories could be an experience of the "dangerous memory of Jesus." We listened to talks by James Martin and Bryan Stevenson and a powerful story-video created by Alicia Keyes imagining what it might look like for a family literally to have to run from a besieged Los Angeles neighborhood and seek asylum along with thousands of other Angelenos at the Mexican border.[8] With each engagement, we asked ourselves, what are we doing and what can we be doing better?

Theologically, we kept close to Metz's injunction to deepen our imaginations about the dangerous memory of Jesus.

What is meant in this context is that dangerous memory that threatens the present and calls it into question because it remembers a future that is still outstanding.[9]

Yes, this quotation from Metz is a bit of a brainteaser for those less familiar with formal theology. I have discovered, however, that with the aid of a simple story, participants can be brought immediately into its prophetic call.

See this with me: You are walking on a warm sun-drenched day. Just beyond you on the same street, two young boys, clearly friends, are walking ahead of you with their arms around each other's shoulders. You hear their laughter and you can only imagine what these best friends are confiding to each other. With their backs to you, you just now begin to take in the strangeness of what you are actually seeing. How is this even possible, you ask? One boy is clearly Jewish, wearing a yarmulke, and the other boy is Arab, wearing a kaffiyeh.[10]

Pause for a moment. Maybe now you feel the prophetic impact of Metz's words and can take in the significance of these questions:

What are the present social, cultural, and political structures that would deny these boys their friendship?

How does the dangerous memory of Jesus call out these structures and "remember a future" for these children?

This exercise at our retreat pushed us to consider the concrete experiences of injustice that are part of our realities. With our stories shared, our experiences named and validated in conversations, we asked ourselves: *What is the future, God's future, that is still outstanding in our Dominican schools*

- *for our communities of color?*
- *for those who identify as LGBTQ+?*
- *for persons forced to leave their homes and livelihoods because of intolerable suffering and oppression by political, economic, and religious systems?*

Then we asked: What is ours to do as Catholic, Dominican educators? What are we already doing to address these social justice demands in our classrooms and among our educational colleagues? What can we learn from each other going forward?

I walked away from this particular retreat thinking: Consciousness is everything—well, almost everything. Coming to consciousness does not guarantee change. In fact, consciousness can rise and fall in our awareness. The discomfort of coming to consciousness can wear on us and draw us away. Too easily, I grow weary of the awareness of my privilege and the constant vigilance of attending to the next step forward. I don't know how I would be able to stay with the work if it were not for my faith and for the community of fellow justice advocates who share stories, resources, and spaces of contemplative restoration.

Now, four years into this ministry, every time I enter a space where I am presenting or facilitating, I am also undergoing the grace I hope to be sharing with others. I am living the journey toward belonging to a community of antiracist, antibiased persons, and I am daily seeking the graces to belong more authentically to the deep story of Jesus. Amplifying *his* story so that the pattern of his life and death can be traced on mine, I hope to become a disciple who more willingly chooses to live, in the words of M. Shawn Copeland, "at the disposal of the cross."[11]

* * *

I returned to my own school where we were making significant strides, engaging our faculty, staff, alums, and board of directors through in-service trainings, conversations, and webinar experiences. And our efforts were having different effects across our school community. Perhaps you have experienced this in-betweenness of justice work, where for some members of your community you have come too late to this party and you cannot make the changes fast enough to suit them, and where others think that we can go back to the way we have always done things after a couple of exploratory but frankly tedious workshops. For me, this was a space of deep discomfort, a space in which I was being stretched daily into the intense and exhausting practice of dialogue that I so matter-of-factly recommend to others. Clearly, I was still on my own journey of aligning my actual behaviors with my inner dispositions of mind and heart, and it continues to be good for me to know how difficult and uncomfortable it is to walk my own talk!

Each week Christina and I, with the support of our two sister administrators, our board chair, and the DJC, plotted next steps toward "progress monitoring" our journey. In June 2021, as we came to the end of that first year together, we could look back and count these important accomplishments:

Five faculty and staff in-services on topics of diversity, equity, and inclusion

Two parent evenings on similar topics of diversity, equity, and inclusion

Support for faculty and staff affinity groups

Three in-service training sessions with the board of directors

Three focus group meetings with student affinity groups

Voices for Veritas and alum circles

Four training sessions for the Dominican Justice Community

The focus group conversations with our student affinity groups were particularly helpful as we came to the end of our first year. Months earlier at one of the parent evenings, one of our dads shared how grateful he was to have a chance to learn about our justice initiatives, particularly about how we were approaching the work of "being on an antiracist, antibias journey." He laughed, sharing that it was his daughter, our student, who had impressed on him that this was important work: "Come on, Dad, you've got to know that you have become an antiracist. We all do." While many of our students shared his daughter's views, the truth was that too many of our students still experienced microaggressions either as people of color or as persons who identify as LGBTQ+.

Given these realities, at first we thought that we should convene a Voices for Veritas "student version" in April or May as the school year was beginning to wrap up. Consultation with our students indicated that they were not interested in such a gathering. However, they were eager to express those immediate actions that would do a great deal to secure a more welcoming and inclusive school climate from their perspective. They asked for simple and clear commitments from us:

Please learn our names.
Please stop asking us to read literature that harms us.
Please notice when you teachers or other students single out a person of color in the classroom.
Please see us in our identity and stop mistaking us for who we are not.
Please provide a recognized, easily accessible, and trustworthy structure for us to report microaggressions.

Our eventual response began with a commitment statement that our principal read publicly to the student body and that we published for our various publics. We committed to addressing the experience of name confusion and found a new software that we implemented schoolwide for all members of our community to record in their own voices the names by which they prefer to be known. Working with our high school leadership team, we initiated a curriculum review that would continue into the new school year, and we continued to provide our teachers with opportunities to reevaluate both their syllabi and their instructional practices. Our commitment "no longer to allow the *N* word to be verbalized in our classrooms" was very significant for our students, parents, and alums of color. And, recognizing that we had not provided a safe channel for students to report harm experienced on campus or at off-campus school-sponsored events, we inaugurated a DEI Student Advocacy Team to enable communication, redress, and repairing relationships. Probably the most significant point made in the commitment statement were these words read by our principal:

> In a special way, I want to acknowledge, welcome, and support our newest Affinity group, our GSA (Gay Straight Alliance), and clarify for all students that we honor and respect our LGBTQ+ students and their allies. You belong to us and we belong to you. Our student activities are welcoming spaces where all students can experience belonging and safety. Students who bring guests to school activities are responsible to inform their visitor(s) of our school's anti-racist, anti-bias culture commitment and the expectations we hold for a spirit of hospitality and respect.

For the greater part, our commitments to our students were well received, and as we turned toward a new school year, one in which we were finally fully able to be on campus again after the worst of the pandemic, we knew that implementing and sustaining these commitments offered us the challenge to remain creative, attentive, and proactive in strengthening the bonds of belonging.

Before leaving for the summer break, we had outlined for the school community the next steps toward which we would be working in the coming year. With the help of an equity educator, we would start the new school year by deepening our understanding of how bias functions in all of us, and how we can address it consciously in learning environments. Departments would continue to unpack how bias shows up in both learning content and processes, equipped with new questions to inform our pedagogy: *What does equity look like in research processes? What does equity look like in grading and student outcome evaluations? In the content taught and the actual classroom space a student enters each day?* We would also explore how to integrate justice and equity questions most effectively in the classroom.

Guided by the antibias education (ABE) curricular structure provided by Teaching for Justice, our teachers continued to develop strategies that support learning outcomes imbued with the justice practices that support our identity as a Catholic Dominican school.[12] And our students were noticing our efforts. Articles in our school newspaper highlighted both our questions and our progress.

By August, we had laid the groundwork among most of our constituencies—particularly with the DJC, our parents, and our students—to begin the coming school year with fresh goals. The DJC started to work on specific language to share with our community about how we define being antiracist and antibias. Our monthly conversations bore fruit, and in February 2022 we were ready to begin convening circle conversations among our constituencies to share, listen, and receive feedback from our greater community. And while this was happening there were new developments on other justice horizons.

I had been in this role for only about three months when I made a call to my friend and TEBT (Theological Education between the Times) colleague Mark Jordan. I had been listening to our faculty and staff at a meeting, and one staff leader had remarked, "I just don't understand what the big deal is about using pronouns. Why aren't we asking people to share their pronouns?" I called Mark. "Can you help me understand this question?" Mark was wonderful and he shared his practice of inviting Harvard graduate students who would like to share pronouns to do so, but only if they wanted to. That was my first experience with approaching a new worldview of nonbinary gender identities.

My next moment was attending a workshop by Luisa DeRouen, a Dominican sister who has been walking with members of the

Catholic transgender community for twenty years. I attended more than one workshop with Luisa, and I hope that in some way I have imbibed something of her amazing pastoral approach to both transgender persons and our Catholic Church. Luisa's profound insight into the incarnational journey of transpersons locates their journey within the paschal mystery of dying to rise to new life. Listening deeply to transwomen and transmen speak of their journeys, Luisa started to see the pattern of Christ's own redemptive journey inscribed on the bodies of the persons she was accompanying spiritually. Telling the story of her experience of walking with persons who struggled to live within a body they felt is not really theirs and then to embrace a kind of death in order to rise up into their true selves, opened for me a whole new understanding of the human mystery. And when I realized that many of the persons Luisa accompanies knew their transgender identity early in life, as mere children, I began to ponder how to provide for such a possible student in our future.

Pronouns were only the beginning of this journey. Whereas inviting faculty and staff members who wanted to share their pronouns publicly could be relatively simple, a more complex situation arises when students at a women's institution ask for this consideration. What does it look like to affirm gender identities and walk with our LGBTQ+ students, particularly our questioning or trans students, when our school's mission is very specifically the education of young women?

The simple practice of naming pronouns uncovered a much deeper and significant question for us, one that could not be answered without engaging with the religious community that sponsors our school. And from my position "in between," I knew that our community's leadership team would need more information, study, and engagement with this question before it could offer a clear, pastoral, and authentic direction. Once again, I felt overwhelmed by the sheer intensity and gravity of what these questions were asking, by the sparsity of a clear Catholic approach, and by the controversial nature of the secular responses on either side of the questions being played out in the media.

Our own GSA (Gay Straight Alliance) students became aware of another local (women's) school's decision to admit only students who were identified "biologically female" at birth. For our small number of questioning students, this news created pain and panic: Would our school do the same thing?

Our escalating justice initiatives continued to produce the mixed reactions of "too much" for one group and "too little" for others, with both groups expressing their displeasure. And while I keep John Lewis's maxim of getting into "good trouble" close to my mind and heart, this is a very painful "in between" for a recovering perfectionist! And just at such moments, when I have felt confounded and so sorrily limited, some poem, prayer, podcast—some resource—comes to me, and it's just what I need.

That is exactly what happened when the email from New Ways Ministry appeared in my inbox.

CREATING A SPIRIT OF WELCOME

A Workshop on Integrating LGBTQ Issues
in Catholic Schools

For Administrators, Staff & Faculty Leaders

Afterward, I would describe this moment to my spiritual director as a sort of culminating confirmation. I told her how I felt: that this partnership with the Divine seems to be inscribing on me a pattern *I might actually begin to trust*. I shared how I am stretched, exhausted, and frankly stymied by the sheer expanse of this work. Yet, I also told her about finding in each day that "one thing" that is needed to step forward. The next day my spiritual director sent me the final stanza of Denise Levertov's poem "The Spirits Appeased."[13] The poet speaks of the Divine's anticipation, that maybe the beloved might finally "begin to see" in the odd coincidences of being provided for the complicities of grace.

These "chance" findings of what is needed in the moment are, I think, actually not at all by chance. When needed, that which is required "appears in my hand, inscribed by yours." It reminds me that I must dwell more often in the unanticipated intimacy of such a sure and tender partnership.

My feeling remains one of immense wonder and humility in the lived experience of grace, not coincidence, meeting me in my desires, my limitations, and my mission to serve *veritas*.

Frank DeBernardo and Robert Shine, codirectors of New Ways Ministry (NWM), created a two-day workshop for twenty of us in the fall of 2021. As I spoke with both Frank and Bob about the possibilities open to us, I realized that this was an important opportunity for more than our school. The Zoom format allowed me to invite leaders from our school as well as our sisters' leadership team and leaders from our sister school (also an all-women's institution) to join us in learning how we, as a congregation, might justify, build, and implement our support for the full inclusion of LGBTQ+ persons from "an authentically Catholic position."

Our NWM moderators began by acknowledging that the ministry in which we hope to engage with our students and employees is controversial. For we live in a time when understandings of what it means to be a gendered human being are contested and politicized. Beyond mere differences in opinion, anti-LGBTQ+ violence is fueled by fear, bias, aversion, and religiously misguided moral judgments.

The experience was truly liberating for our participants—but not without challenges. It reminded us that, as Catholics, two significant moral traditions guide our understandings of what it means to live whole and holy lives: Catholic social teachings and Catholic teachings on sexual ethics. We also learned that these two traditions are presently in a kind of "tug of war."

The tension between these traditions runs through many church documents and often is expressed in some sort of variant of this formula:

The church protects the human dignity of LGBTQ people and condemns all kinds of unjust discrimination against them. AND the church also teaches that sexual activity between people of the same sex is not morally permitted. AND/OR the church believes that people's gender identity is determined by the sex, either male or female, assigned at birth.[14]

New Ways Ministry goes on to report that a remarkable development in recent teaching is the emergence of a "small hierarchy" that places the social justice tradition over the sexual ethics tradition. As early as 1983, the bishops of the Washington Catholic Conference stated that "prejudice against homosexuals is a greater infringement of the norm of Christian morality than is homosexual . . . activity." Working with this and other teachings that direct our church community to embrace the blessing and gift of our LGBTQ+ members in an environment of "respect, compassion, and sensitivity," our school and congregational leaders directed me to begin to plan for an expansion of our relationship with New Ways Ministry.[15] In February 2022, our faculty and staff had two workshops with NWM, and in March we invited leaders of our parent organizations and our board of directors to a special evening presentation conducted by Frank and Bob.

Keep in mind that such moments can be both difficult and challenging for a community. When I wrote to our employee community about our engagement with New Ways Ministry, I wondered what responses my email would elicit. The letter started with my adapted translation of Micah 6:8, "This is what God asks of you, only this. That you act justly, that you love tenderly, and you walk humbly with your God." After sharing the particulars of what to expect and how to prepare, I then said this:

As Frank, our NWM presenter, pointed out to our November participants, stepping into this important work is controversial. The amount and intensity of anti-LGBTQ+ rhetoric and activity expose deeply held biases that are too often fueled by religious messaging. Our goal is to educate our community in VERITAS, the truth that all people are God's people, precious, beloved, and chosen for life in its fullness. Our mission compels us to take a long, loving look at what is real and then to act justly.

Stepping into this work is also a commitment. We are on a journey that is already asking us to deepen our clarity of mission and this involves our entire community: parents, students, alums, the board, and our sponsor, the Dominican Sisters of Mission San Jose. I want to acknowledge that this NWM workshop with our employee community is a moment on our whole community's "growing in justice" journey. There are many more of these moments still ahead of us.

One response we received led me to send a second message to our employee community. A staff member with a great heart for this work asked what provisions were in place for our LGBTQ+ members who would be taking in difficult teachings such as that homosexual activity is "objectively disordered"?

I could have kicked myself! After all the work I had been doing in circles and in creating brave spaces, I had missed a significant pastoral moment. The justice journey drops me daily into a humility that calls for both honesty and self-compassion.

I share this because you also may find that despite all your attention to detail, the sheer volume of antibias, antiracist initiatives catches you off guard and you either succumb to old efficiency patterns or simply fail to see what is missing. When I confessed my misstep to Christina, she wisely reminded me, "Sister Colleen, that's why we have a community." With my colleague's feedback, I crafted a second preparatory message to our community.

Dear Colleagues,

As we prepare to gather tomorrow for our first New Ways Ministry workshop, I would like to encourage all of us to review [our] Norms for Conversation. Our sisters have adopted these norms as practices for right relationship among us as Dominican Sisters, so it is good for us as a sponsored ministry to continue to reflect on them and regularly consider them in our meeting spaces and our classrooms.

Use I statements.
Listen to understand, not to respond.
Own your intention and your impact.
Approach conflict constructively.
Be mindful of your participation.

Expect mistakes, discomfort, and lack of closure.
Maintain the privacy of those who share out loud.

For tomorrow, I want to reinforce and name the norm, "Be mindful of your participation." As I shared in an earlier email, this work is controversial and can be the source of strong feelings: uncomfortable or difficult for some, inspiring and uplifting for others. We all will want to attend to how we are participating in our bodies.

Stay close to these questions:

- *What am I feeling and thinking as I listen to the presenters?*
- *Do I need to practice self-care by stepping back, breathing, and possibly going off camera for a space of time?*
- *On the other hand, am I hearing things that disturb my past understandings and certainty of church teaching? Can I breathe and lean into my feelings of discomfort and gently release the temptation to shut down or shut out what is being shared?*

Our desire is to grow in our shared mission together. Thank you for embracing this opportunity to grow our capacities to hold brave space together.

All good,

S. Colleen

Perhaps you're wondering how it went. Well, for the most part I think that it was received relatively well. The struggle, and therefore the opportunity to practice how to "approach conflict constructively," remains. How do you foster among a community (in this case, our diverse employee community) a sensibility for what it means for an ecclesial community to work through a living question, a disputed moral question? How can we argue fiercely and kindly at the same time? This is exactly what our Dominican tradition of *quaestiones disputatae* is all about. In our highly polarized context, we encounter culture warriors on both sides of the divide; folks whose attachment to certainty threatens to override their commitment to stay in relationship. Fania Davis, whose personal justice journey awakened her identity as a warrior-healer, recounts:

> I learned about restorative justice—a justice that seeks not to punish, but to heal. A justice . . . that is not about getting even, but about getting well. A justice that seeks to transform broken lives, relationships, and communities, rather than shatter further. . . . Learning about this new but ancient justice marked a climax in my own years-long movement towards wholeness. It provoked an epiphany, integrating my inner warrior with my inner healer and uniting the opposites within: fire/water, solar/lunar, masculine/feminine.[16]

I am only beginning to understand the gift of Fania Davis's integration and how it speaks to what other justice advocates are sharing, and to the ancient wisdom of my own Christian contemplative tradition.[17] I can be reactive to the triggers of others; I have my own attachments to certainty. I am not immune to these downward-spiraling energies. Learning how to stay steady in the conflict with a heart poised to listen deeply for the truth-in-process pushes me to seek resources for spiritual resilience; resources and relationships (friendships!) that constantly stretch me to open myself to the mystery of our fundamental human oneness.

In March we expanded the New Ways Ministry workshops to include the leaders of our parent community and our board of directors. The information was clearly new to a significant number of our participants. Not unlike what occurred with the original engagement with NWM in November, the information shared challenged and reordered perceptions of Catholic moral teaching. And both the complexity of emerging gender sciences and the variety of pastoral responses worldwide brought home to all of us that we are in the midst of a new question about what it means to be human, and that only with an attachment to the Holy Spirit guiding our living tradition can we hope to expand the circles of belonging and human flourishing.

Going forward, we recognize that the important responses ahead of us involve training two significant lenses on our school's mission. As a school with a storied history of educating women, we have long articulated a commitment to single-gender education as a gift that empowers our students and offers them as a promise to our world and its future. As our whole school community and our sponsor, the Dominican Sisters of Mission San Jose, continue to learn more about gender science, we will want to look again at our mission of educating young women and allow our justice learnings to inform and animate our next steps forward.

The groundwork remains to be done. The young people who are with us presently are already questioning and seeking spaces where they can be who they are with confidence and security. As we work to reclaim what it means to live our mission as a single-gender institution, we must also create the spaces that will allow us to come together and listen deeply to our students and explore with them how we can more concretely secure their ability to grow into their whole and best selves. The Spirit has clearly confronted us sisters as we reflect on past practices with regards to our LGBTQ+ students. Recognizing now that former unspoken policies, amounting to "don't ask, don't tell," compounded the harm that our LGBTQ+ students endured, we realize even more deeply how we failed to meet the moment for our students. We failed to walk with them in their questing humanity, to know how to be themselves before God and creation. We abdicated that journey to kind colleagues, often of other or no faith traditions, and thus reinscribed the awful false message that "there is no welcome for you, as you are, in our church community." Grieving this truth, even though we might have been personally significant to a single LGBTQ+ student, we hold responsibility for contributing to a climate that fostered fear, anxiety, and hiddenness. And when some of our LGBTQ+ students, in their alienation, engaged in overt challenges (public displays of affection [PDA], constant uniform violations, etc.), our fear turned to judgment, deepening the chasm between us. They became the "difficult" students we could hardly wait to graduate.

Today, we recognize that we are entering into what Bishop Pierre Claverie, OP, one of our recent Algerian martyrs, called the broken spaces, the *lignes de fracture*, the fissures in our social world, caused by human sin and oppression. We must step into these "lines of fracture," those spaces of pain, owning our participation and impact, expressing contrition, and working to heal the harm.

The break, the fissure for us in our archdiocese, has been a very public history of denial and lack of support for LGBTQ+ persons. For years prior to my arrival here, GSAs were not allowed in archdiocesan high schools. Our lesbian students had to form a stealth club that students learned about only by word of mouth. Religious studies faculty recall the callous ridicule expressed on the topic of LGBTQ+ students and curricula at archdiocesan meetings. We did not challenge; we kept our place; we allowed the dominant perversion of our Catholic teachings to perpetuate the lie that LGBTQ+ persons are immoral people. We participated in the smog of fear, rejection, and judgment within the Catholic community toward LGBTQ+ persons.

In abdicating our formative role in the lives of our LGBTQ+ students, we essentially invited them to seek other sources of life and spirit. And while, because God is God, there are plenty of alternative places readily available and open to them, we who claim to serve a God of infinite, self-donating love withheld that treasure from God's beloved children. This is a major indictment and one that we must, with God's merciful forgiveness and grace, address with all honesty and an undaunted attachment to *veritas*.

Conversations are beginning with our GSA (now QSA, Queer Student Alliance) and with religious studies faculty and others who want to help us create spaces for healing and affirmation. At the core of this effort is our clear and undivided commitment to serve the spiritual and emotional flourishing of our students. Inviting our students to deepen their sense of respect and care for their unique human journey, we seek to open spaces for them to integrate their passions of mind, heart, and spirit; treasure how they were created to love; and offer them a vision of a full and life-giving future. Clearly, we want to teach as Jesus *does*.

Episode 6

Becoming

If your faith makes you ready . . . renew now the vows of your own baptism.

Reject sin; profess your faith in Christ Jesus. This is the faith of the Church.

—From the liturgy for baptism

"Reject sin; profess your faith in Christ Jesus." These invitations to witness to our faith cannot be meditated upon long or deeply enough. It is Easter Sunday 2022 as I write these words, and when Father Larry led us in the ancient profession of baptismal faith this morning, I heard these words with a new urgency and pathos. For the world is broken in so many ways, and there is such a deep longing in our communities for a sustainable peace and a lively hope. Yet for all that brokenness and longing, it is also painfully clear that some of the breakdowns have needed to happen. To quote Paul Tillich, some of the disruptions are very much "shaking the foundations" of our invisible and sinful social structures and are crying out for us to put our bodies where our faith is and to stand against evil—to reject sin.

It was not that long ago that I caught a glimpse of this invisible sinful structure through an ordinary encounter that it would have been easy to dismiss. I was sitting in the audience of the opening session of the Catholic Theological Society of America (CTSA). I was sitting right in front of the venerable scholar M. Shawn Copeland, of whom I had only heard, being myself merely ABD (all but dissertation) at the time. The practice of the CTSA is to invite the bishop of the diocese in which we are meeting to welcome and address the membership at the opening assembly. The archbishop of this particular city stepped onto the podium to rousing applause as he was also a well-established and respected theologian in his own right. I enjoyed his talk, which at one point offered us a verbal picture of the rich diversity of the archdiocese. Group by group, he named the immigrant peoples who pioneered this city and how they contributed to the richness of the local Catholic church he shepherded. And then he sat down.

From behind me, I heard Shawn Copeland exclaim words along the lines of, *"Oh no! Not again! NO! Not again! We don't exist. We are not seen! We are not recognized! Yet again!* **Why can't our own church see us!?"**

I was as guilty as the prelate. I realized in that moment how I, too, had failed to see or name the gifts and pastoral contributions of Black Catholics in all the spaces in which I had lived and ministered.

Today, I look back and recognize that the "smog of racism" produced a deep "color blindness" in me. If I had not heard what I did, *heard Shawn's pain, anger, and disbelief expressed so genuinely*, I would have missed completely the prelate's disconnect with his own people. I would have remained as oblivious to my color blindness as he was to his.

As I continue to study Black Catholic history, in our schools, in our parishes, in our convents, and in our seminaries, I see a history of remarkably faithful Black Catholics who have the tenacity to resist over and over again the experience of ecclesial erasure by a white church. Ours is a forgotten sinful history of racial violence in which we relegated black bodies to the last pews and often refused them the body of Christ at communion rails and in communion lines.

I remember the story that a Black elder shared at a listening circle sponsored by a local Catholic college following the murder of

Michael Brown in St. Louis. We sat together, six women—four white, two black—and we listened. This is the story the elder shared:

I was a new Catholic. This was in the 1940s, and I was going to Arkansas to visit my family there. My family knew I had become a Catholic and they helped me to find the local parish where I could go to Mass on Sunday. At communion time, I knelt at the rail. When it was my turn to receive communion, the Father went on past me. He did that over and over, as others knelt by me, received communion, and returned to their pews. The Father was skipping me. I kept kneeling until I was the only one left kneeling and then he gave me communion. When I walked out of that church, the Father called me over and told me that I was never to come to that church ever again.

I had read about stories like that of this gentle elder, and now I was a witness. A younger white woman sitting next to me in our small group was utterly dumbfounded. She had never known or witnessed overt anti-Black bias toward fellow Catholics within their own church.

Too many Catholics are like this young white woman. We need such stories to bear prophetic witness to how deep, pervasive, and hidden is the racialization of our United States Catholic experience. But even more, we need these testimonies as monuments to the "uncommon fidelity" of Black Catholics.[1]

When religious orders refused entrance to Black women, women like Mother Mary Lange found a way and created their own communities of vowed women religious of color.[2] When United States seminaries refused Black men entrance, men like Augustus Tolton sought ordination in Rome and returned to minister in our church. When Black laity were told to find their ecclesial home elsewhere, primarily in Black Protestant churches, lay Catholics like Daniel Rudd convened "Colored Catholics . . . for the purpose of taking the status of the race in their relation to the church." Rudd's efforts toward convening "Colored Catholics" from 1889 to 1894 began what is today the National Black Catholic Congress. At the conclusion of its fourth congress in 1893, members published a summary statement that, as a kind of "theological meditation," affirmed their attachment to a church that "has labored to break down the wall of race prejudice, to teach the world the doctrine of the meek and humble Christ." And bravely, such faith-filled Black Catholics also publicly called out their fellow Catholics who deny their common faith by departing "from the teaching of the Church in the treatment of the colored Catholics and yield[ing] right to popular prejudice."

> As children of the true Church, we are anxious to witness the extension of our beloved religion among those of our brethren who as yet are not blessed with the true Faith, and therefore we consider it a duty, not only to ourselves but to the Church and to God, that we draw the attention of every member of the learned Roman hierarchy to such violations from Catholic law and Catholic practice.[3]

It is not truthful of white Catholics to deny or diminish the social, historical, and cultural biases described above. It is not truthful of us to deny or diminish how this evil *calls our true Catholic identity into question*. At a time when the politics of left and right dominate our spaces, we Catholics must instead return over and over again to the gospel of Jesus Christ and listen to his Spirit speaking to us about right relationship and how that looks among the baptized. Caught in structures into which we were born, we cannot claim a "free pass" simply because we, personally, did not create the structures that continue to privilege so many of us. We are not absolved from the responsibility of living as Christ would among us even now. As Christians, his mystery is our mystery, his story is our story, his way of living and dying is ours as well. That's what we say our immersion into the waters of baptism has done to us: it has marked us for life, for Jesus's life, for his way of being and doing.

Can you tell? Can the world tell? *How is the indelible identity mark of baptism showing up in our community in our time?* Can you see it in how we are actively rejecting sin?

Structural sin is real, and the searing truth is that these world-forming structures are the spaces in which our desires and appetites are trained and cultivated, desires and appetites that are counter to the gospel of Jesus. Here's the insight (from Richard Rohr) that has me reeling:

> If we don't nip evil [of structural sin] in the bud at the level where it is legitimated and disguised, we will have little power to fight it at the individual level.[4]

I am not ignorant of structural sin as a concept. I have read and studied about the reality of structural bias for many years. Rohr's insight, however, has turned my imagination of the causal relationship between the structure and the individual on its head. My imagination had long been like that of many others, and it went like this: If you can convince individuals to be better humans, then the corporate sin will go away. In other words, like many of my fellow Catholics, I had a stronger investment in personal conversion, good works, and the pursuit of holiness than I had in paying attention to racist power structures and systems that secure my comfortable space in the world (at the expense of many others' space).

So words like Rohr's, and Copeland's, and those spoken at the Fourth Black Catholic Congress of 1893 confront me anew with how to dismantle the dehumanizing structures that nice people don't see. They confront me with how to approach that quite sincere, devout Catholic mother who explained to me recently that she is not a racist. She shared her growing discomfort with our school's public affirmation of being on a journey to become an antiracist, antibias school community. The words "antibias" and "antiracist" had hit her hard. She heard them as an accusation. From her perspective (and others who have been speaking to me), "antiracist" presupposes a previous condition of "being racist," of consciously choosing to be a racist. That is not a personal identity that she can own. She explained to me, "Sister, I am a welcoming person, I am not a racist. In fact, whenever a Black family comes to Mass, I go out of my way to say 'hello' and 'welcome to our church.'"

When conversations get to this level, I know that we have a very long way to go. No, I have that wrong: *I know that I have a long way to go* because *I* too am still learning how to interrupt with love.

As a One on the Enneagram, "a Reformer," I have no issue with helping you to see where you can improve. As a "reformer" type, that's my gift to you. However, as you can well imagine, people are not very responsive to being told they are obtuse, stupid, or misguided. In fact, just this week my daily EnneaThought reminded me to observe the One's "strong tendency . . . to try to improve" my partner, family, and friends with my "rationality."[5] There is an inherent judgment that, given the force of my personality, can communicate harshness and condemnation. That is why, as a theologian-formator, I continually work at how to deliver the message without evacuating it of its power.

An image that comes to my mind is that of Ieshia Evans, the Baton Rouge nurse who stood her ground as she was being rushed by Louisiana State Police during a peaceful protest condemning police violence in both Minnesota and Louisiana. In fact, during this past Advent, I paired the image of Ieshia Evans with that of Our Lady of Guadalupe as a way of inspiring our students to connect the consequential parallels between these two women and their choices for life. Separated by time and space, they are "sisters" in their choice to accept a call that both women recognized as divine action in their hearts. As Ieshia explained later, "Sometimes jobs are given to you that you don't apply for." I intentionally linked Ieshia's words with the image of Mary of Nazareth in her appearance to the indigenous people of Mexico as *Nuestra Senora de Guadalupe*, who also took a stand for the people of Tepeyac.

This dimension of the work of relating our Christian revelation and teaching to real life and the pressing questions of our times together goes to the heart of my Dominican theological vocation. What I love about our Dominican incarnational perspective is the *most certain conviction* that God meets us in the wide range and expansive scope of our embodied lives. This was the genius of Dominican theologians Yves Congar (1904-1995) and M. D. Chenu (1895-1990), who were deeply troubled by the way the Roman Catholic Church of their day dismissed the tumultuous struggles happening in society, politics, and philosophy and retreated into a defensive, self-protective ecclesial shell. Because these two men had drunk deeply at the wellspring of the tradition and understood its promise and power to sustain every generation of believers, they were able to contribute mightily to the Copernican shift in Roman Catholic theology that made possible what became the Second Vatican Council. Recent comments made by prominent ecclesial leaders calling into question the wisdom of the church's engagement with secular movements would seem to be a retreat from the dialogical commitments made at Vatican II. When I think such thoughts, I recall that every social movement, be it secular or religious, will be incomplete and limited in its liberative fulfillment. For our commitments are not to idealized utopias but to the cries of God's beloved people on a life journey that, for too many, is far too short. In the crying out and the listening, we attend to reality as it is, and we take the next step for justice. Both Saint Catherine of Siena and Black Lives Matter know the power of crying out for justice.

> Silence is violence.
> —Black Lives Matter

> Preach the Truth as if you had a million voices.
> It is silence that kills the world.
> —Saint Catherine of Siena

Speaking out to name and dismantle structural sin does, in fact, require a "million voices"—Catholic voices, Muslim voices, Jewish voices, Sikh voices, Protestant voices, evangelical voices, secular voices. Without our mutual engagement in the struggle to expose, resist, and, when necessary, tear down the dehumanizing constructs of our times, we ourselves are at risk. If we cannot call out "white privilege," if we cannot recognize it as the by-product of racism, if we cannot resist the temptation to remain defensive and offended by the demands for justice in our times, we succumb to more than those hidden structures of oppression: we become active participants in them. We participate in "sanctified, romanticized, and legitimated violence," historically unleashed in those moments when human communities conclude that such violence is necessary to control and contain the threats to their power and position.[6] We have only to look at what happened in Washington, DC, on January 6, 2021, to recognize how the "powers, principalities, thrones, and dominions" of which Paul of Tarsus spoke in his letter to the Ephesians (6:12) can seduce our imaginations and compromise our commitment to the Great Commandment of Jesus: our love of God and love of neighbor.

So, however it is received, I may not and shall not stop teaching and preaching that we white Catholics are compelled to grow the spiritual and emotional capacities to become antiracists. When Ibram X. Kendi says that it is not enough to be nonracist, he is absolutely correct. And Shawn Copeland is correct too: We Catholics have another history here in the United States, one that we rarely teach in our schools and from our pulpits. If we are truly to become the body of Christ in our time, we will commit to developing the spiritual strength and exercising the moral courage that acknowledge the harm that we through our complicity, silence, and inaction have inscribed on our ecclesial body.

What would our church look like if we white Roman Catholics apprenticed ourselves to the remarkable faith journey of the Black Catholic community? Might we encounter the amazing grace of our Black sisters and brothers' "uncommon faithfulness," their mighty and tenacious resilience of spirit, and the profound depth of Black joy?

> I believe in God. I hope in God. I love.
> I want to live and die for God.
> —The Venerable Henriette Delille

* * *

Unsurprisingly, my most recent initiatives with our parents and employees have centered on learning how to link the language of antiracism to our Catholic social teaching in a creative way.

Earlier in the past year, our Dominican Justice Community (DJC) wrote a draft statement of what it means for our school to be an antiracist, antibias institution. After practicing how to conduct circle conversations with restorative practice principles, our DJC members were ready to hold space for the constituencies of our communities. At this writing, we are still inviting our community to learn more about how our descriptions of being antiracist, antibiased evolved, and we are receiving their feedback. Here's a summary of our working definitions:

> Antiracism is the intentional work of actively opposing racism as expressed in racial hierarchies, embedded in structures, policies, and practices. This journey is different for each person depending on one's unique background and life experience; however, we all breathe "the smog of racism," and we choose to drive our decision making by purposefully partnering with and amplifying voices from historically marginalized and oppressed groups. *If we are not actively embodying veritas and working to combat racism, then we are complicit in perpetuating racism.*
>
> Antibias is the intentional work of recognizing that we all have implicit bias (stereotypes and attitudes) associated with categories of people. Implicit bias can support and sustain structural inequities (such as classism, sexism, anti-LGBTQ+ beliefs). And these implicit biases can intersect and harm persons at multiple levels of personal identity. *In order to embody veritas, an antibias approach requires purposefully identifying, confronting, and challenging our individual and institutional biases.*
>
> Antiracism and antibias are commitments that happen on individual, interpersonal, institutional, and structural levels. We have a collective responsibility to embed these practices in our school. We will know that we are making

progress when the diversity of our student body is reflected in our faculty, staff, and board of directors and when our curriculum aligns with culturally responsive educational practices. *Embodying* veritas *within an environment that is antiracist and antibias would mean that every member of the community belongs and is supported, and no one feels the need to leave or change aspects of their identities.*

Our working definitions will evolve. They are meant to, as we grow in our commitment and uncover more dimensions to our healing and opportunities for accountable engagement.

When Christina and I introduced our initial conversations about race and bias with the DJC, we selected two different resources to support our thinking. One resource is a continuum to which I was introduced while working with our faculty at my previous school. Crossroads Ministry has been supporting the work of racial justice and healing in church communities for many years. Their continuum has been a mainstay for me as I engage in this work among our sisters' various ministries. Perhaps you have encountered this resource in your own journey as a pastoral theologian or preparing others for pastoral ministry. Take a moment and consider each of the columns below that describe the elements associated with the antiracist, antibias institutional journey. These behavioral descriptions get at what the journey looks like concretely. They remind me of the right relationship map (Episode 3) and how a community benefits from naming specific examples of what real progress looks like on this justice journey.[7]

Does this figure make you wonder where your primary community might land on Crossroads Ministry's continuum? Doing this exercise can be an engaging and productive type of corporate examen. Take a moment now and review each of the columns. Consider them prayerfully before coming to any judgment about your organization. Stay with your experience. What statements best echo how you experience your community's antiracist, antibias journey? (And it's okay if you discover, as I have in the past, that you are resonating with statements *across* the continuum more than with statements in one single column. That's data, too.)

Stay with your assessment: What are you seeing? What are you wondering? What interpretations are you drawing from this exercise? With whom might you share your observations?

I have seen the continuum used in different contexts and with different groups. My most positive experience with the tool has been in the classroom, introducing students to the idea of assessing a ministry's alignment with its justice mission. Students were curious, open, and transparent in their assessments. I have found that when using the continuum with members of the same community, establishing norms of conversation up front is essential. I've also learned that when there is limited knowledge among participants, say, convening a group of parents within a school community, it is critical to establish a brave "container" or setting in which a variety of experiences can be expressed—all the more so when members with diverse life experiences weigh in on how they view the organization's location on the antiracist, antibias continuum. Naming for the group, at the beginning of the exercise, that two seemingly opposite experiences can be true at the same time supports a tone of mutual respect without denying the presence of discomfort.

We discovered this last important insight when we were acknowledging and repairing the harm named in the @dear Instagram posts addressed to our school. Sitting with stories and the variety of experiences named, both good and difficult, teaches me that people don't experience the same reality in the same way. Even more, within a single person two very different things can be true at the same time. For instance, I can say that I loved my time teaching in academia and I can also recount profoundly hurtful experiences from which I continue to heal. Both are true for me. What about you? What memories and realities does this raise for you?

Our conversations about where we find ourselves as a Catholic Dominican school in terms of the continuum were eye-opening.

CONTINUUM ON BECOMING
AN ANTI-RACIST MULTICULTURAL ORGANIZATION

Monocultural → Multicultural → Anti-Racist → Anti-Racist Multicultural

Racial and Cultural Differences Seen as Deficits → Tolerant of Racial and Cultural Differences → Racial and Cultural Differences Seen as Assets

1. Exclusive *An Exclusionary Institution*	**2. Passive** *A "Club" Institution*	**3. Symbolic Change** *A Compliance Organization*
• Intentionally and publically excludes or segregates African Americans, Native Americans, Latinos, and Asian Americans • Intentionally and publicly enforces the racist status quo throughout institution • Institutionalization of racism includes formal policies and practices, teachings, and decision making on all levels • Usually has similar intentional policies and practices toward other socially oppressed groups such as women, gays and lesbians, Third World citizens, etc. • Openly maintains the dominant group's power and privilege	• Tolerant of a limited number of "token" People of Color and members from other social identity groups allowed in with "proper" perspective and credentials • May still secretly limit or exclude People of Color in contradiction to public policies • Continues to intentionally maintain white power and privilege through its formal policies and practices, teachings, and decision making on all levels of institutional life • Often declares, "We don't have a problem." • Monocultural norms, policies and procedures of dominant culture viewed as the "right" way, "business as usual" • Engages issues of diversity and social justice only on club member's terms and within their comfort zone	• Makes official policy pronouncements regarding multicultural diversity • sees itself as "non-racist" institution with open doors to People of Color • Carries out intentional inclusiveness efforts, recruiting "someone of color" on committees or office staff • Expanding views of diversity include other socially oppressed groups *But . . .* • "Not those who make waves" • Little or no contextual change in culture, policies, and decision making • Is still relatively unaware of continuing patterns of privilege, paternalism and control • Token placements in staff positions: must assimilate into organizational culture

4. Identity Change	5. Structural Change	6. Fully Inclusive
An Affirming Institution	*A Transforming Institution*	*Antiracist Multicultural Organization in a Transformed Society*
• Growing understanding of racism as barrier to effective diversity • Develops analysis of systemic racism • Sponsors programs of antiracism training • New consciousness of institutionalized white power and privilege • Develops intentional identity as an "antiracist" institution • Begins to develop accountability to racially oppressed communities • Increasing commitment to dismantle racism and eliminate inherent white advantage • Actively recruits and promotes members of groups that have been historically denied access and opportunity *But . . .* • Institutional structures and culture that maintain white power and privilege still intact and relatively untouched	• Commits to process of intentional institutional restructuring, based upon antiracist analysis and identity • Audits and restructures all aspects of institutional life to ensure full participation of People of Color, including their worldview, culture, and lifestyles • Implements structures, policies, and practices with inclusive decision making and other forms of power sharing on all levels of the institution's life and work • Commits to struggle to dismantle racism in the wider community, and builds clear lines of accountability to racially oppressed communities • Antiracist multicultural diversity becomes an institutionalized asset • Redefines and rebuilds all relationships and activities in society, based on antiracist commitments	• Future vision of an institution and wider community that has overcome systemic racism and all other forms of oppression • Institution's life reflects full participation and shared power with diverse racial, cultural, and economic groups in determining its mission, structure, constituency, policies, and practices • Members across all identity groups are full participants in decisions that shape the institution, and inclusion of diverse cultures, lifestyles, and interest • A sense of restored community and mutual caring • Allies with others in combating all forms of social oppression • Actively works in larger communities (regional, national, global) to eliminate all forms of oppression and to create multicultural organizations

Clearly we had areas of strength, spaces where we have been working and growing. If I had to name one space that will remain a growing edge for our community, it is our location as a PWI, a predominantly white institution. Unlearning whiteness as a PWI is going to take us years. It reminds me of the experience we first had with the @dear Instagram postings. As a Catholic, Dominican PWI, we had yet to recognize truly the structures of privilege that support and animate energies of exclusion and experiences of diminishment for historically marginalized and minoritized persons and communities. We perceived ourselves as sincere in our desire to serve God's people generously and selflessly. We worked very hard to make this education available to more and more families in need of financial support. We actively recruited a diverse faculty, staff, board members, and students. Even so, we had yet to interrogate deeply how our location in a PWI town seeps into our own social and cultural expectations and practices. We are only beginning to acknowledge the significant and multiple stumbling blocks for BIPOC and to create a plan for how to remove those barriers.

Data really helps to support the kinds of culture changes we are seeking. Organizations like the National Association of Independent Schools offer, assessment tools to measure the experience of belonging across the constituencies of a school environment. We recently offered the AIM (assessment in multiculturalism) climate survey to our school community, and our DJC is beginning to work with the data that survey produced. This step is important because without the courage it takes to provide feedback spaces for all members of the school community, we lose out on the opportunity to see ourselves as others perceive us. Remember, "*Veritas* is not a goal, it is a standard." Standards call for regular evaluation. If we are going to implement the right relationship map faithfully, we have to discover the tools that will allow us to do both personal assessment and communal measurement toward the standards we hold as a school.

One of the challenges I am finding in myself and in the community is the tendency to become defensive and devolve into what I am recognizing as a "blame culture." There are diverse dimensions of the blame experience running across our social/cultural locations. As I was thinking out loud about this, Christina pointed out a defense mechanism I had not yet perceived: white defensiveness and feeling personally blamed for racial harm. The way it works is that a white person expresses the feeling of undeserved blame for a social system they did not create. It can go like this, "I am being made to feel uncomfortable in my own skin; you are implying that being white is bad or evil." Or, from the perspective of a school situation, "My child comes home and tells me that they feel that being white skinned is a problem." Deeper interrogation of such claims might actually show how the defense mechanism of projecting (this sense of being unfairly blamed) functions preemptively to mitigate action for justice. By projecting my white guilt, I effectively halt the process of facing the evil consequences of racialized outcomes and disparities.

Beyond this experience of blame, I asked myself and our community: What else is getting in the way of us becoming a more genuinely just school community? Contemplating some of the interactions of the past two years, I started to consider what a "systems approach" might contribute toward dismantling institutionalized racism and bias within our school. Why? As we began to sort through events, policies, and procedures identified as problematic in terms of equity and inclusion, I noticed in our community a reluctance, a reticence, and a general feeling of fear of making mistakes. Even now, there remains a sense that most, if not all, of our people want to learn and grow, but that something is holding us back. Frankly, as a learning institution we were hesitant to be learners. Such hesitance looks like this:

- I don't know how to intervene.
- I am afraid I will overstep my role.
- We really need guidelines to help us do this well.
- I don't want to try this in my classroom because, what if I don't do it correctly?
- It's too risky to make mistakes in a school like this.

What if our culture were a true "learning community" culture? What would support this growth mind-set among all of us, all our constituencies? One recent article on the topic helped me organize my thoughts about my experiences these past two years.[8] Marilyn Paul's insights into the difference between blame and accountability got me to think about how a blame culture insidiously functions to undermine human learning processes, which always involves experiences of missing the mark or making mistakes. When a blame culture is functioning fully, it is hard to imagine how to take new risks, because if you don't do it right the first time there are indeed major consequences. However, such consequences in a blame culture don't serve the mission of the community. Their only function is to name (read "shame") the failure by searching out and identifying "the problem." Blame stops there. *We think we know what or who went wrong. We say it's their fault.* In contrast, a learning culture is an accountability culture. The focus is on learning, not merely on ascribing fault.

When I read Paul's description of an accountability culture, I knew I had stumbled upon an important insight that might help our ongoing Mission DEI initiatives promote a comprehensive sense of our shared journey in becoming basically better humans. This is what she wrote:

> Becoming aware of our own errors or shortfalls and viewing them as opportunities for learning and growth enables us to be more successful in the future. Accountability therefore creates conditions for ongoing, constructive conversations in which our awareness of current reality is sharpened and in which we work to seek root causes, understand the system better, and identify new actions and agreements. The qualities of accountability are respect, trust, inquiry, moderation, curiosity, and mutuality.[9]

Here was another dimension of quality relational living that aligns with our commitment to becoming more adept at living from restorative consciousness. Practicing accountability as described above raises the bar on the quality of our interactions.

We, as leaders and together with our DJC, have an important role to play in growing fresh capacities for demonstrating accountability, and for helping our community to stop our habit of blaming. To do so, we will need to model, speak about, and share across our community the values and behaviors that will nurture a growth mind-set among all of us. What I feel excited about as I write this is the fact that Paul's insight that accountability invites us to "seek root causes, understand the system better, and identify new actions and agreements" aligns perfectly with our antiracist, antibias commitments to do just that.

* * *

Two conversations, one with a teacher and the other with a small group of mothers, challenged my own capacities to practice the dialogical disciplines of right relationship. Upon reflection, these are helpful occasions that remind me how much more practice I need to grow and strengthen my "dialogical muscles." In the moment, depending on what is said and how it is communicated, I can quickly forget the restorative practices and norms of conversation by which we have agreed to live as a community. As I think about it from a distance, I recognize that I struggle with points of view that I deem deeply lacking in the experience of proximity.

What do I mean by that? If a person's circles of encounter are small and tight, without real engagement with experiences unlike their own, then the opinions they express can lack significant connection to the other's reality. Ideas are so much easier to debate than another person's real life. Devoid of any real encounter with "the other," it is so much easier to engage in philosophical discussions about lives other than our own and even to engage with the other person's humanity.

This can be particularly frustrating when those who resist our justice work refuse to engage or even consider the resources that we offer for their consideration and have purposefully designed to bring us all closer in our shared humanity. I ask questions like: *Were you able to join us for the New Ways Ministry workshop in sup-*

port of our LGBTQ+ community? Have you had a moment to watch the video we created to introduce our working definitions of becoming "antiracist" and "antibias" in the Catholic tradition? When the response is no, my frustration escalates, and I struggle to stay connected in the conversation. I am still learning how to breathe when folks get dug in. I recognize that this is when I really struggle to model the values I espouse and the behaviors I am trying to make my own. I struggle to choose to remain in that space of discomfort with a generous ear. I meet my own reactivity and my own "fundamentalisms." I really have to work to see myself as I am in that moment. I am just as "hooked" or activated as the persons who are disagreeing with me, and I am quickly slipping away from listening into defensiveness.

As you can imagine, these listening sessions are not for the faint of heart. If we are authentically attempting to walk in the light of *veritas*, then we are necessarily attending to all the levels of engagement that are happening within and among us simultaneously: tone, body language, narrative, eye contact, emotion, and breath. I am becoming more practiced in the art of attending to both the lens through which I am viewing the encounter and the interior mirror that is showing me who I am in that moment. All of that matters in trying to be an agent of the reign of God in that moment.

* * *

Years ago, in one of my graduate ecclesiology classes with a group of health-care mission students, we got into a wonderful conversation about the skill sets needed to be a mission leader in an ecclesial ministry. Specifically, we were reflecting on the experience of mission leaders as the "frontline interpreters" of the Christian tradition for their ministry. I loved introducing my students to the gifts of our tradition, those gems of ecclesial wisdom that can animate and guide our engagement with a whole range of questions that arise from just being human. In the light of all the possible threats to our fragile and brief existence on the planet, how do we demonstrate to others—specifically to those in our health-care setting—the love that we have come to know in the God revealed in Jesus?

Pope Benedict said, "Mercy is in reality the core of the Gospel message; it is the name of God."[10]

It is hard to think of a space in which bodies matter more than a health-care facility. It is a space in which the need to know the mercy of God is most desired and sought. Here, medical professionals make life-and-death decisions daily, and mission leaders support the institution in its accountability for those decisions. It is not easy work, and at times good people disagree and find themselves culling the tradition to support their positions. Dialogical spaces in an ethics committee meeting can get squeezed tight at times, particularly if the ministry's relationship with the local bishop is strained. Knowing all that, one of my students had a brilliant insight during that class session. "Our next degree should be in diplomacy!" Indeed! Learning how to lean into the human situation of the present moment with skillful listening, patience, and a capacity to communicate across strained differences such that all involved recognize that they are being heard and engaged is a critical skill for a church that desires to be "a field hospital" in a deeply troubled world.

I needed such a skill set when our school president called me and shared that, given the leak of the *Dobbs* Supreme Court decision, the ruling that overtuned *Roe v. Wade*, students and faculty were asking for guidance about responding to the situation, particularly about the possibility of participating in public protests around the pending decision. "Could you please write a statement of clarification of our Catholic position and offer guidelines for going forward?" It took me two days to work out that statement of clarification with guidelines for our faculty and staff. I admit that the process of writing had an effect on me, a clarifying effect. So often when it comes to such profoundly difficult moral questions, we forget to honor the fact that they are questions, ones that require prayer, deep listening, and ongoing dialogue. So as I wrestled with the thinking and writing, it became clear to me that a one-sided response, a response that ignores the real struggles and underlying issues represented by those who believe otherwise, would not honor our commitment to stay in the conversation. What prompted that realization was the late Cardinal Joseph Bernardin's articulation of the "seamless garment ethic."[11] It gave me a way of holding the questions surrounding *Roe v. Wade* with clarity and compassion.[12] I then found words from Pope Benedict to that same effect:

> Dialogue without ambiguity and marked by respect for those taking part is a priority in the world and the church does not intend to withdraw from it.[13]

Here's what I eventually wrote for our administrators to share:

Dear Colleagues,

Once again current events have drawn our community into a profound struggle that challenges our mission to live an authentic human life with faith, integrity, and truth. Our Catholic tradition teaches that when significant human questions arise we must listen deeply, respectfully, and then act for justice, according to our informed consciences. We believe that this dialogical process, challenging as it can be, opens a space for both veritas and compassion. A model of this intentional discernment is the gift we offer to our young women at this moment.

As a Catholic Dominican school we believe and teach that every human life, from its beginnings in the womb to its completion in death, is to be respected, treasured, and protected. We also realize that for women, childbearing is a remarkable commitment and that too many women, particularly women of color, face pregnancy without the real supports that honor their dignity as human beings.

As our country works through the current crisis of the future of Roe v. Wade, we affirm our school's Catholic commitment to the "seamless garment ethic" for all human life, from beginning to end, and confirm our shared responsibility to uphold our Catholic moral teachings, particularly the dignity of all human life.

Even among Roman Catholics there is a diversity of opinions about this topic and how we hold both the care of the mother and life of the child in mutual dignity. For those who might like to come together and talk through their thinking and wonderings about this challenging social question in a spirit of dialogue, let's meet Wednesday at 2:50.

Requested Guidelines

We have been asked to offer guidelines to support full transparency regarding our school's expectations during this time. We offer these guidelines as an initial clarification of expectations. We remain open to any questions of clarification that may emerge going forward. We share this in a spirit of humility as we seek to live the charism of veritas together.

1. *We respect each person's constitutional right to participate in public protests. Should you as an employee choose to participate in protests regarding Roe v. Wade, we ask you not to wear any garment (hats, T-shirts, sweats) or carry any signs that bear our school logo/name or any recognizable symbol that would identify you as a member of our school's community.*

2. *We ask that you not publicly promote or invite students to participate in protests regarding Roe v. Wade.*

3. *If your social media accounts are open and accessible to our parents and students, please refrain from messages that are in direct opposition to the moral teachings of the Catholic Church concerning the dignity of all human persons.*

4. *In classrooms and gatherings with students (co-curricular and informally) we ask that you represent the moral teachings of the Catholic Church clearly and in a spirit of dialogue. This is an opportunity to enact the norms of conversation with which we have been working in our justice initiatives.*

Again, we invite interested faculty and staff who would like to share more about these guidelines to meet with us on Wednesday at 2:50.

I received gratitude for this communication from various members of our community, including members of our board of directors. Being myself an intuitive, I have to say that I felt a communal sigh of relief among us since the release of this statement. In responding as quickly as we did to that request from our faculty, I learned how important it is to offer direction and spaces for conversation when those are requested. These "interruptions" that rearrange and stretch our work agendas and responsibilities we ignore at a cost. The sense of calm we have as a result of offering clear and compassionate clarification is worth all the effort to create that communication.

When the DJC meets for its final gathering this school year, we will welcome new members, review our progress to date, and set goals for the coming year. Along with welcoming our first director of diversity, equity, and inclusion in August, we will plan our review of the AIM survey data and discuss how, together, we might best create a climate of positive curiosity and compassionate commitment to address our expanding opportunities for growth: all the learning curves of our becoming an antiracist, antibias Catholic Dominican school.

Yesterday, as I reflected on our school, I began to imagine in my mind's eye the webs of relationships that constitute our "system." There's the academic life of our school with all the relational dynamics of teacher-student, faculty-staff-administration, and how we organize and evaluate ourselves to create the best possible educational experience for our students. There are all the support services, from facilities to finance, that make the smooth delivery of our classroom and school activities possible. There are those whose presence enhances our learning environment by providing for the emotional and physical well-being of our students. There is our campus ministry and service programs that are poised to provide our school with the spiritual resources needed by all of us entrusted with safeguarding, promoting, and embodying our mission daily. There are all those who support our students in the cocurriculars and sports, the visual and performing arts. And there are those amazing folks who make life for our resident students a safe and happy home away from home.

All these webs of human relational connection matter in our justice journey of becoming an antiracist, antibias Catholic Dominican school. All these relationships constitute opportunities to reflect on how we are systemically expressing our commitment to *veritas*. Together, for better or for worse, we are the bodies, called to live *veritas*, so that this small, amazing school can be what it is and reach for what it can yet become.

Episode 7

Futuring

For surely I know the plans I have for you, says the
LORD, plans for your welfare and not for harm, to give
you a future with hope.

—Jeremiah 29:11 NRSV

I have pondered Jeremiah's words several times in the last couple of years as I stepped into this personal and professional in-between time. Returning to that precious memory of an initial Spirit invitation to *"step away, Colleen, turn from the closed door and meet me in a vast, new and verdant space"* to the memory of going there, I know that the God of Jeremiah's promises meets me still. I have walked into that vast and verdant place, met new folks, and learned words and ways to speak of this amazingly faithful God. Words and ways that, both bold and humble, might be received and pondered.

> "Sister Colleen, I really like that phrase you just said, 'contemplative pause'; I'm going to use that!"
> "Sister, I cannot tell you how much I appreciate the language of 'right relationship.' I wish the school would create a guide for parents so we can have these conversations about right relationship with our children."
> "Sister, this is why we send our daughter to this school. We

want her to be in an environment in which she experiences what it is like to strive to align one's actions with one's values and beliefs."

Truly, I never anticipated the transformational journey of this almighty push into "the between" of academic theology and pastoral practice that began with a quite unexpected pink slip. Three years on, what would I say now about the journey? That this is the only way of doing theology that matters. Just today I participated in my third New Ways Ministry in-service, introducing another group of secondary teachers to the work of creating a Catholic welcome for LGBTQ+ people. In so doing, I once again experienced the power of doing theology on the ground. My ecclesiologist friends would have had a field day listening to us (baptized Catholics) grapple with the tension between our Catholic justice tradition and our Catholic sexual ethics, teasing out the multiple understandings and imaginations of "the church" at play in our conversations. Today, I bless the God who allows me the privilege of naming that we, "the church," are already here, already present, and already pastorally engaged in witnessing to God's mercy in our schools.

So, I look back at that "pink slip" moment today, the one that sent me out of the traditional classroom, and I am profoundly grateful: grateful for the amazing grace and mercy that, even now, meets me, sustains me, and humbles me as it generously works on me and my community. *Grace will have its way with us, right? Grace is relentlessly opening us to our future, our hope.*

As I continue to offer to the circles of ministry presently entrusted to me the gifts of theology, I hear new questions, and I am learning how to engage those questions as *she who accompanies.* I have a special memory of Robert (Bob) Schreiter of Catholic Theological Union saying that the work of theology is not about providing answers but about how to walk with a community, equipped with a theological "toolbox" at the ready, to assist the community in its own articulation of faith. I now know what Bob meant, and I could not agree more. Theological education is about midwifing the faith that wants to be born out of the questions that have made some kind of ultimate demand on us, questions that will not let us go, because something new wants to come to life. To abandon the questions, to refuse to engage their complexities, or to answer the question prematurely and definitively is to endanger the new life gestating among us. Here, I know I am channeling some amazing Dominicans (Marie Dominique Chenu, OP; Yves Congar, OP; Edward Schillebeeckx, OP; Pierre Claverie, OP) who have gone before me. They have taught me by their practice of theology to love the questions that life offers, because there, at the intersection of faith and life, grace awaits. The privilege—mine and yours—is to hold the question, to empower critical theological reflection on our current practices, and to sustain the bonds of communion.

Back to the questions:

> "Sister, I am struggling with how this institution is both 'Catholic' and 'empowering of women.' I do not understand how to put those two together. Can we talk?"
> "Sister, can we gather a group to plan how to use Catholic social teaching more effectively in public support of our LGBTQ+ students?"
> "Sister, can we partner with the Admissions Department and identify what obstacles prevent Black families from choosing our school for their daughters?"

Such questions are opening new opportunities for me and my colleagues to go deeper in faith and institutional integrity. Those opportunities are where "the rubber" of grace meets "the road" of our lives. Grace is *for* all of us. Grace is *always on our side*, attentive, present, and real. Grace bears transformative, curative powers. If we choose "the way" of right relationship, then grace empowers us to embody *veritas*. For in this justice work, *the medium is the message*. Unless I apprentice myself to the demanding and humbling practices that restore and heal relationships, I am frustrating God's hopeful plans for my future—and for our future.

Personally, the grace of good theology has recently sustained me once again during a time of unanticipated trial and upheaval. Following an injurious experience with my own community of sisters, I found comfort and challenge by daily returning to special "nuggets" of theology that soothed my wounded spirit. Here are a few favorites:

The face of God whom we seek is already turned towards us.
—Catherine Mowry LaCugna[1]

If we do not transform our pain, we will most assuredly transmit it— usually to those closest to us. . . . Scapegoating, exporting our unresolved hurt, is the most common storyline of human history.
—Richard Rohr[2]

Silence is God's first language. Everything else is a poor translation.
—Thomas Keating[3]

Early in my journey of healing, I found that silence was my dearest refuge. For in the silence I could own my suffering, my anger, my sense of disorienting loss. In the silence I could begin to grapple with the challenges of embodying *veritas* as a daily decision to step into the paschal mystery as it was approaching me in this fractured moment. With time and therapy, my anger is resolving into grief, and that is where I am now. I find it to be a kind of spiral experience as part of which new encounters with my community elicit yet-to-be-healed pain. And as spirals go, I find that I arrive at new and freer spaces as I practice leaning into the lessons of grief rather than trying to avoid them.

Perhaps you, too, have experienced such suffering in your personal life.

Going forward for me means a return to the roots of my Dominican vocation. What is the pearl of great price for which I must, once again, cull the field? What is the pearl of great price I need to reclaim as mine in order to continue with this group of both fabulous and flawed human beings? (Tell me, is there any other kind of human?) Step by step, I am making my way. Step by step, I am walking a restorative way that invites me to meet grace at the deepest level of soul so as to align my values for reconciliation and healing with my practice.

It is hard work! It is exhausting work. And it is liberating work—as assenting to "undergoing God" can be if I embrace this opportunity as graced action carving out space in me by subtraction. "Let go to let come" is a new mantra I intone when I feel old energies of blaming and shaming overshadowing my spirit. So I let go of blame and hurt, and instead attempt to approach with reverence that which is as it is.

* * *

When I wrote above that the decision to embody *veritas* is a decision to accept the daily rhythm of the paschal mystery in my life, I did so without drama or sentimentalism. I now have a fresh desire to step toward the future with an approach of reverence toward whatever in the past I yearn to control. In a real sense, that desire to step forward with reverence comes only after a profound emptying of my spirit. Looking back now, I can only marvel at how mercy found me one day at a time, and how each time it brought me through. I heard it expressed this way recently: *Pain brings us to the crossroads. Love pulls us through.*[4] Perhaps you too will find those words helpful.

* * *

Back at school, August 2022 found our community embracing several "firsts." We welcomed our first ever director of diversity, equity, and inclusion, a direct outcome of the justice work initiated in those last two years. We came together, as faculty and staff, for the first time with a sense that COVID-19 was more evidently in our rearview mirror. And for the first time we returned to school preparing to welcome more than forty new colleagues in a variety of positions, several in senior leadership roles. Like many if not most educational institutions, we were managing the challenges and opportunities of the "great resignation," a pandemic-era phenomenon in which approximately 50.5 million left their jobs in 2022.[5] Such seismic shifts in an organization can leave you wondering about your future.

I met with our new colleagues to share our school's mission and our commitment to living in right relationship. The general climate among our newest employees was strongly positive; they shared gratitude for the chance to contribute to our educational mission. One new teacher shared, "Sister, I have always hoped to join this school's faculty. When this opportunity opened, I could see it only as God's invitation." Particularly at a moment in which I was grieving the departure of a number of the colleagues who had been committed to our Mission DEI initiatives, these words of my newest colleague, expressed so genuinely, invited me to step into this new moment with deep trust. *The folks who are meant to be here are here. Take the next step together. The future is what we will create together.*

And that future in most ministerial communities, like yours and mine, I think, is one in which we don't seize enough opportunities to have fun together. Many of us are seriously "fun deprived." It was my dear TEBT colleague, Willie Jennings, who first brought the idea of "Joy Work" to my attention. What a gift! With almost half of our school community new to our mission, what an opportunity for a fresh moment of mission-centered community building! It was time for us to create some laughter, joy, and merriment together. Partnering with my colleague, Juli James, director of community life, we plotted a day of fun, connection, and reengagement with our mission. Do you know who in your community loves cats more than dogs, and vice versa? We do! We discovered who our mountain versus beach folks are, as well as our coffee versus tea drinkers. As Juli guided us, I watched joy lift us as a community. I witnessed mutual hospitality as old and new members stepped into the fun of the moment. Who would imagine how simple activities like "force choice" (i.e., you can only choose one, coffee or tea) could help foster new bonds of camaraderie and welcome?

Juli's enthusiasm and energy for creating a gracious space of joyful connection for our community inspired and buoyed me. Yes, I admit to being both initially stumped and spiritually depleted regarding how to invite our faculty and staff into an appropriate contemplative space, a container, if you will, that could hold all of us, new and old alike. Once we've set the tone with creative welcoming processes and community-building activities, how do we go deeper together, build a new institutional foundation in trust, and claim our mutual commitment to living the school's mission together?

I have already shared with you how I encountered grace on this in-between journey. Well, this time, I literally met grace in the form of a book, sitting on our president's desk: *The Five Graces of Life and Leadership* by Gary Burnison.[6] And while Burnison's text is not overtly theological, his reflection on **G**ratitude, **R**esilience, **A**spiration, **C**ourage, and **E**mpathy offered values that I knew would enliven a reflective exercise about what it means to live in right relationship in our Dominican Catholic institution.

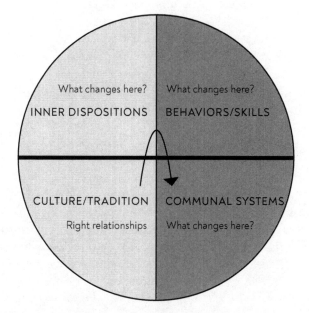

So, using the right relationship map, we oriented our community once again to the significance of being a place where faculty, staff, and administration "walk their talk" personally and support the larger values that animate our school culture.

Earlier in our gathering I had left copies of a document on the tables, entitled "Our Commitment to Mission." We also created a poster of the statement and displayed it in the room from the outset. Here's what it said:

OUR COMMITMENT TO MISSION
2022–2023
BEING IN RIGHT RELATIONSHIP WITHIN,
AMONG, BEYOND

Right relationship, as reflected in Catholic social teaching, is
the state of being in
which our inner dispositions of mind and heart for
wholeness, healing, generosity, and graciousness
are in alignment with our actions.
Living out of right relationship is a daily commitment of making
the gospel of inclusive love and reconciling restorative practice
the center of our being and our doing.
As a community, we commit this year to amplify our practices
of belonging through
honest encounter, genuine dialogue, and evident inclusion,
as we continue our justice journey empowered by
God's love.

Remember what I said earlier about my own recent difficult patch in my journey into restorative practice with my sisters? I wrote the above statement only two weeks into my own healing process, my new apprenticeship to those very restorative practices. Yes, I was "running on empty," and look what came out of that! Could it be that those words came not "in spite of" but precisely "because of"? What if by setting out on my journey of integration, some fruit of the journey arrived for my ministry? It is worth pondering in faith.

In the end, might not the best gift, the tenderest lesson in theology that we offer our students, be the witness of our own willingness to step with intention into moments of transformation, even knowing they'll often include suffering and self-emptying?

We had a good retreat. We—faculty and staff—resonated with the activities and generously engaged with the reflective process, mutually sharing the attributes of grace that we recognize live in us. Identifying those virtues individually and then experiencing through a gallery walk the density of the virtues embodied in our community set the stage for the final invitation: to sign the commitment statement poster together.

So now it's your turn. How do gratitude, resilience, aspiration, courage, and empathy find a home in you?

Gratitude

Resilience

Aspiration

Courage

Empathy

Take a few moments, and then use the space above either to jot down in words or to draw what your own experience of these words has been. When have you experienced these virtues? With whom do you associate these capacities of spirit? How do you relate to these words as possible verbs that fuel your life?

Next, review the virtues of grace listed on page 148 and consider the quotations associated with each.

G The *G* in "Grace" is Gratitude: "If the only prayer you said was thank you, that would be enough" (Meister Eckhart, OP).

R The *R* in "Grace" is Resilience: "If your heart is broken, make art with the pieces" (Shane Koyczan).

A The *A* in "Grace" is Aspiration: "The greatest danger for most of us is not that our aim is too high and we miss it, but that it is too low and we reach it" (Michelangelo).

C The *C* in "Grace" is Courage: "Courage is the most important of all the virtues because without courage, you can't practice any other virtue consistently" (Maya Angelou).

E The *E* in "Grace" is Empathy: "Be kind whenever possible. It is always possible" (Dalai Lama).

(Inspired by *The Five Graces of Life and Leadership*
by Gary Burnison)

Consider each of the virtues of GRACE and rank it according to how well-practiced you feel you are in each. For instance, you might select E as your first or top-ranking virtue, because you know that empathy is the strongest of the five virtues in your life. Try to stay close to what you know to be true of yourself, rather than what you wish would be true of you. What are you noticing in your list? Did you have any ties?

I hope that an exercise like this supports your vision of who you want to be in your life and ministry. And before you turn the page, perhaps take a moment to consider what other virtues of yours come to mind as you reflect on your own journey of spiritual maturity and living into right relationship, and what other virtues might represent your growing edge.

* * *

Drawing these reflections to a close, I thank you for stepping into my "in between" as a theological educator. Maybe you have resonated with parts of my journey. I imagine that most of us theologians experience being "in between" at one time or another. As you may have come to see, becoming a "frontline interpreter of the gospel" invited me into a profound learning curve, one that continues: How will I continue to bring the gifts of theology to a ministry, to a community, to *my* community? That "becoming" happens with each new question concerning the human mystery that presses upon the ministry, the community, asking, "What about this?" What about Catholic identity? What about the human misery at our borders? What about transforming a PWI into an antiracist, antibias institution? What about queer Catholics? What about . . . ?

What will be our future questions, yours and mine? The lesson I am learning in this "in between" affirms that answers are less helpful than accompaniment. That whenever the next assault on human dignity or the latest revelation of social sinfulness comes to light, our way forward is just that—a walk, an accompaniment, a relational way, sourced in grace and practiced in reconciliation. Sourced in grace, our ability to accompany each other in *veritas* is possible because we are held by the divine promise of accompaniment: "I am with you always" (Matt. 28:20). The "always" of this promise invites an intimate and dynamic relationship between humanity and God. Initiated into it while still in our mothers' wombs, we are held in life by a singularly faithful God. I am meeting anew this fidelity, this sense of "being held," as I navigate life's contingencies. Our life's journeys transcribe on our persons the power and the potentials of this relationship. And this is not despite our finitude or sinfulness, but a result of the covenant of grace that our ridiculously generous God lavishes on each person. Graham Greene had it right: "You can't conceive, my child, nor can I or anyone, the appalling strangeness of the mercy of God."[7] Each of us will have the opportunity to express and reexpress in our flesh, should we choose, the ultimate truth of our being: we are God's own beloved.

> *Being the Beloved constitutes the core truth of our existence.*

We can embody such grace because it is God's gift to us to do so. The transformative capacities and outcomes of attempting to do good theology do not exist in some other-than-human space in between heaven and earth. The fruits of the Spirit of which Saint Paul writes *require* human bodies: bodies that bend in reverence and stretch forth in peace and reconciliation; bodies that see goodness and express kindness in a tender glance; bodies that touch with healing and withstand in forbearance (Gal. 5:22–23). These fruits of the Spirit can only be known and experienced through the agency of human beings: people who make their own the revelation of an incarnate God. People who take the truths manifested in Jesus the Christ for us and break them open. People who in their very bodies become an encounter of divine mercy alive in the world. People like you. So how do you embody divine mercy and *veritas* in these in-between times?

For Further Thought

1. Go back now and consider your responses to the reflection questions and exercises offered throughout this book. What are you noticing about yourself, your institution, and your community? Take time to consider how you speak and think of your contributions to the work of theological education. On reflection, is there anything you would like to do differently? What do you (or your institution) need in order to live into those changes? Whom would you invite to partner with and accompany you?

2. Consider the other books in this Theological Education between the Times series. Which of these titles might challenge and support your own journey as a theological educator seeking to embody *veritas*? What groups within your community or institution could you convene for deep reading and conversation for action?

3. What is your most recent experience of a "pink slip" moment—your own or someone else's? For those of us who have experienced such moments, "metabolizing" grief is

one of the most significant dimensions of living into a future imbued with hope. I highly recommend that you read Francis Weller, *The Wild Edge of Sorrow: Rituals of Renewal and the Sacred Work of Grief* (Berkeley, CA: North Atlantic Books, 2015).

Notes

Episode 1

1. T. S. Eliot, "Little Gidding," in *Four Quartets* (New York: Harcourt, Brace, 1943).

2. James Alison, *Undergoing God: Dispatches from the Scene of a Break-In* (New York: Continuum, 2006).

3. David Richo, *Five Things We Cannot Change . . . and the Happiness We Find by Embracing Them* (Boston: Shambhala Publications, 2006).

4. Online memorials, like "Stitch Their Name" and "Know Their Names," attempt in some small way to document and memorialize those lost to anti-Black violence. See respectively https://tinyurl.com/yrc2s938 and https://tinyurl.com/yc7v2u3r.

5. José Antonio Pagola, *Recuperar el Proyecto de Jesus* (Madrid: PPC Editorial, 2015), 31. Translation by Tere Maya, CCVI.

Episode 2

1. Dr. Martin Luther King, *Letter from Birmingham Jail* (San Francisco: HarperSanFrancisco, 1994).

2. Grace Sandman, "@dear Instagram Accounts Prompt Painful Discussions, Public Disclosures about Elite Private Schools," Global Student Square, July 22, 2020, https://tinyurl.com/mwtp7huu.

3. See the PBS interview with Beverly Daniel Tatum, part of the PBS presentation "Race: The Power of an Illusion," accessed August 18, 2023, https://tinyurl.com/me8fy62c.

4. See Peggy McIntosh, "White Privilege: Unpacking the Invisible Knapsack," Working Paper 189. "White Privilege and Male Privilege: A Personal Account of Coming to See Correspondences through Work in Women's Studies" (1988), by Peggy McIntosh; available for $4.00 from the Wellesley College Center for Research on Women, Wellesley, MA 02181, and M. Shawn Copeland, "Constructive Proposal: Body, Race and Being," in *Constructive Theology*, by Serene Williams and Paul Lakeland (Minneapolis: Fortress, 2005).

Episode 3

1. Direction Statement, Dominican Sisters of the Queen of the Holy Rosary, Mission San Jose, CA, 2016.

2. Pope Francis, "On Fraternity and Social Friendship (*Fratelli Tutti*)," October 2, 2020, Papal Archive, the Holy See, https://tinyurl.com/4w3mxujf.

3. Pope Francis, "Address of His Holiness," Ecumenical and Interreligious Meeting with Young People, Skopje, North Macedonia (May 7, 2019), in *L'Osservatore Romano*, May 9, 2019, 9, https://tinyurl.com/3xzyx3s2.

4. Mary Oliver, "The Summer Day," in *New and Selected Poems* (Boston: Beacon, 1992), 94.

5. Marilyn McEntyre, *Make a List: How a Simple Practice Can Change Our Lives and Open Our Hearts* (Grand Rapids: Eerdmans, 2018).

6. David Benner, *Soulful Spirituality: Becoming Fully Alive and Deeply Human* (Grand Rapids: Brazos, 2011), 142.

7. Benner, *Soulful Spirituality*, 142.

8. "In a world of victims, little can be known about a person simply because he calls himself a believer or a nonbeliever. It is imperative to know in which God she believes and against which idols she does battle." Jon Sobrino, *The Principle of Mercy: Taking the Crucified People from the Cross* (Maryknoll, NY: Orbis Books, 1999), 9.

9. Thomas Merton, *No Man Is an Island* (New York: Houghton Mifflin Harcourt, 1955), 150.

10. Clifford Geertz, *Interpretation of Cultures: Selected Essays* (New York: Basic Books, 1973), 68.

11. David Tracy, *Plurality and Ambiguity* (Chicago: University of Chicago Press, 1994), 37.

12. James Baldwin, "As Much Truth As One Can Bear," *New York Times Book Review*, January 14, 1962, https://tinyurl.com/48dxyndm.

13. Mary Douglas, *How Institutions Think* (Syracuse, NY: Syracuse University Press, 1996), 112.

14. Richard Rohr, *Just This* (London: CAC Publishing, 2017), 82–83.

Episode 4

1. Fania Davis, *The Little Book of Race and Restorative Justice: Black Lives, Healing and US Social Transformation* (New York: Good Books, 2019).

2. Pope Francis, *The Church of Mercy: A Vision for the Church* (Chicago: Loyola Press, 2014), 128.

3. Learn more about the National Equity Project here: https://tinyurl.com/ycekwtup.

4. Russell Vought, "Memorandum for the Heads of Departments and Agencies," September 4, 2020, https://tinyurl.com/56eu8n6z.

5. David Benner, *Soulful Spirituality: Becoming Fully Alive and Deeply Human* (Grand Rapids: Brazos, 2011), 50.

6. Cornel West, *Brother West: Living and Loving Out Loud* (Carlsbad, CA: Smiley Books, 2010), 232.

7. Yves Congar, *I Believe in the Holy Spirit* (New York: Crossroad, 1997), 2, 39 (emphasis mine).

8. Benner, *Soulful Spirituality*, 10.

9. Benner, *Soulful Spirituality*, 10.

10. Pierre Claverie, OP, "Humanity in the Plural," in *Pierre Claverie: A Life Poured Out* (Maryknoll, NY: Orbis Books, 2007), 259.

11. These original norms of conversation were shared by Christina at the first faculty/staff in-service in fall 2020. As Christina's slide indicated, they represent her ongoing interpretation and integration of norms for conversation adapted from the poem "An Invitation to Brave Space" by Micky Scottbey Jones and and the work of Stephen Covey. I remain indebted to Christina for her wise selection and integration

of resources in support of our antiracist, antibias justice work. The International Institute for Restorative Practice (iirp.edu) is one such significant resource. The IIRP also provides resources in languages other than English. For information about Christina Hale-Elliott, see Elliott Educational Services (https://tinyurl.com/46pae56z).

12. See Andrew Weil's 4-7-8 Breath Relaxation Exercise, Andrew Weil Center for Integrative Medicine, the University of Arizona, accessed September 26, 2023, https://tinyurl.com/yccxtayh.

Episode 5

1. Pierre Claverie, OP, *"Lettres et messages d'Algérie"* (Paris: Éditions KARTHALA, 1996), 22–23 (my translation).

2. Fania Davis, *The Little Book of Race and Restorative Justice: Black Lives, Healing, and US Social Transformation* (New York: Good Books, 2019).

3. My favorite resource for this conversation is the aforementioned book by David Benner, *Soulful Spirituality: Becoming Fully Alive and Deeply Human* (Grand Rapids: Brazos, 2011), and I often invite participants to spend time with Benner's descriptions of both healthy and toxic spiritualities.

4. James Martin, *Building a Bridge: How the Catholic Church and the LGBT Community Can Enter into a Relationship of Respect, Compassion, and Sensitivity* (New York: HarperCollins, 2018).

5. Martin, *Building a Bridge*, 15.

6. See the Catechism of the Roman Catholic Church, paragraph 2358. https://tinyurl.com/2fbs3f4z.

7. Learn more about Marian Social Justice Initiative at https://tinyurl.com/yk9f3ywr.

8. See *Spiritual Insights for LGBT Catholics*, by Fr. James Martin (https://tinyurl.com/3mzjc773). "We Need to Talk about an Injustice," a TED talk by Bryan Stevenson, https://tinyurl.com/mszhf4s6. "Let Me In—We Are Here," by Alicia Keyes, https://tinyurl.com/4j8c3hxx.

9. Johann Baptist Metz, *Faith in History and Society: Towards a Practical Fundamental Theology* (New York: Crossroad, 1980), 200.

10. To clarify, our consideration of a hoped-for future is a first engagement with Metz's understanding of "dangerous memory." Ted Smith reminds us that "dangerous memory" as expressed by Metz is predicated on the capacity of memory to see through the erasing devices of the present order, recognizing that "the way things are" requires the exclusion of certain others deemed broken and expendable.

11. M. Shawn Copeland, "To Live at the Disposal of the Cross: Mystical-Political Discipleship as Christological Locus," in *Christology: Memory, Inquiry, and Impact*, ed. Anne Clifford and Anthony Godzieba (Maryknoll, NY: Orbis Books, 2003), 177–96.

12. Teaching for Justice, formerly known as Teaching Tolerance, was founded by the Southern Poverty Law Center and participates in SPLC's mission "to be a catalyst for racial justice in the South and beyond." https://tinyurl.com/2zjhum4m.

13. Denise Levertov, "The Spirits Appeased," in *Breathing the Water* (New York: New Directions, 1989).

14. Francis DeBernardo, "Next Steps: Catholic Church Teaching about Prejudice, Discrimination, and LGBTQ Civil Rights," New Ways Ministry, July 28, 2000, https://tinyurl.com/3s9t6vea.

15. The Catechism of the Catholic Church, 1994, section 2358: "They must be accepted with respect, compassion, and sensitivity. Every sign of unjust discrimination in their regard should be avoided."

16. Davis, *The Little Book of Race and Restorative Justice*, 14.

17. Thanks to our amazing consultant, I have been recently engaged with the work of Dr. Shawn Ginwright. See his *The Four Pivots: Reimagining Justice, Reimaging Ourselves* (Huichin, unceded Ohlone Land a.k.a. Berkeley, CA: North Atlantic Books, 2022). And a recent blogpost from the Center for Action and Contemplation introduced me to the work of Rev. Dr. Jacqui Lewis, *Fierce Love: A Bold Path to Ferocious Courage and Rule-Breaking Kindness That Can Change the World* (New York: Harmony Books, 2021).

Episode 6

1. See M. Shawn Copeland, ed., *Uncommon Faithfulness: The Black Catholic Experience* (Maryknoll, NY: Orbis Books), 2009. See also Cy-

prian Davis, *The History of Black Catholics in the United States* (New York: Crossroad, 1990).

2. See, in particular, Shannen Dee Williams, *Subversive Habits: Black Catholic Nuns in the Long African American Freedom Struggle* (Durham, NC: Duke University Press, 2022).

3. Excerpted from the address of the Fourth Black Catholic Congress, 1893. Cited in M. Shawn Copeland, "Tradition and the Traditions of African American Catholicism," *Theological Studies* 61, no. 4 (2000): 632, https://tinyurl.com/4x5nv2ns.

4. Richard Rohr, adapted from Richard Rohr, *Spiral of Violence: The World, the Flesh, and the Devil* (Albuquerque: Center for Action and Contemplation, 2005), accessible at https://tinyurl.com/ys2chjhr.

5. The Enneagram Institute, Ennea Thought for the Day, Type One, for May 3, 2022.

6. See again Richard Rohr's reflection: https://tinyurl.com/ys2chjhr.

7. Learn more about the work of Crossroads Ministry at https://tinyurl.com/5b8mby6p.

8. Marilyn Paul, "Moving from Blame to Accountability," Systems Thinker, accessed August 30, 2023, https://tinyurl.com/yc8rw3su.

9. Paul, "Moving from Blame."

10. Benedict XVI, (2008) *Regina Caeli*. Retrieved from https://tinyurl.com/5a6s29kd.

11. In 1983, Cardinal Bernardin, then chair of the US bishops' pro-life committee, gave a pivotal talk that challenged the Catholic ethical imagination toward "a single, consistent ethic of life at every stage and in every circumstance," effectively connecting as whole a "seamless garment" in protection of all threats to human life: specifically but not limited to abortion, poverty, nuclear war, and euthanasia.

12. Cardinal Joseph Bernardin, "A Consistent Ethic of Life: Continuing the Dialogue" (William Wade Lecture Series, St. Louis University, March 11, 1984), https://tinyurl.com/mrhe8hy8.

13. Benedict XVI, "Meeting with the World of Culture," May 12, 2010, https://tinyurl.com/zjs94tdb.

Episode 7

1. Catherine Mowry LaCugna, *God for Us: The Trinity and Christian Life* (New York: HarperCollins Publishers, 1991), 331.

2. Richard Rohr, "Transforming Pain," Center for Action and Contemplation, October 17, 2018, https://tinyurl.com/2z5jmcjn.

3. Thomas Keating, *Invitation to Love: The Way to Christian Contemplation* (London: Bloomsbury Publishing Plc, 1992), 105.

4. Ted Dunn, *Graced Crossroads: Pathways to Deep Change and Transformation* (St. Charles, MO: CCS Publications, 2020).

5. Greg Iacurci, "2022 Was the 'Real Year of the Great Resignation,' Says Economist," CNBC, February 1, 2023, https://tinyurl.com/3trt8me8.

6. Gary Burnison, *The Five Graces of Life and Leadership* (Hoboken, NJ: Wiley & Sons, 2022).

7. Graham Greene, *Brighton Rock* (London: Penguin Books, 1943), 268.